A Country Childhood

Other books from Red Post
Smugglers' Trails
Cherries First Hundred Years

A Country Childhood

Boyhood Memories of
Victorian Rural Dorset

Written and illustrated by
H.S. Joyce

edited by
Roger Guttridge

RED POST

First published in 2000 by Red Post Books
© Red Post Books 2000

A CIP catalogue record for this book is available from
the British Library.

ISBN 1-901533-23-9

Red Post Books
The Old Warehouse
32 Gloucester Road
Bournemouth
BH7 6HZ

Telephone +44 (0) 1202 252144
Fax: +44 (0) 1202 246370

Red Post Books publish illustrated non-fiction books. If you have a title
which you think may be of interest, we would be pleased to hear from
you. You should address your enquiry to the Editorial Director at the
above address.

Contents

H.S. Joyce the angler

Introduction

The Reluctant Banker

Roger Guttridge introduces Harry Joyce: author, artist, angler, naturalist

NTIL 1994, I had never heard of H. S. Joyce, which on the face of it is surprising given the common ground in our respective professional and geographic backgrounds, albeit two generations apart. It is stranger still that it took a Yorkshireman to introduce me to this most interesting of Dorset's sons, an eccentric and multi-talented character who wrote and illustrated seven books on rural life and angling and countless articles for the leading country and country sports magazines of his day.

In February 1994, Mark Bedford, of Farsley, Leeds, telephoned me in the hope of learning more about the man whose writings had inspired his own love of angling and the countryside. Mark, who was given H. S. Joyce books as a small boy, told me: 'I virtually taught myself to fish from his books. Now I'd like to find out what happened to him and his tackle and to trace his son, who I believe is still alive.'

Mark had already been in touch with the National Trust who, coincidentally, were at that very time following their own line of research on H. S. Joyce in connection with their plans for his birthplace, White Mill at Sturminster Marshall, which they intended to restore and open to the public. The historic millhouse had been bequeathed to the Trust by the Honourable Ralph Bankes thirteen years earlier together with the rest of the 16,000-acre Kingston Lacy and Corfe Castle Estates in Dorset.

National Trust researcher Keith Eldred had already discovered that the Joyce family were at White Mill from about 1550 until the early 1900s. They ran the mill, farm and bakery, all of which are referred to in Joyce's books, although the property had ceased to be a water mill after the dam burst in 1865. 'After that the milling was reduced in favour of baking and farming,' said Keith. By 1891 the Joyces were living in Rowlands Hill, Wimborne, although still associated with White Mill.

The 1891 census return shows their address as Oaklands, Rowlands Hill. The head of the household was Shapwick-born Thomas D. Joyce, aged 49, a farmer. His wife was Ellen, aged 42, who was born in Wimborne. Like their father, the five eldest children were all born in the parish of Shapwick in which White Mill lies, despite its proximity to the village of Sturminster Marshall. The children were Margaret, aged ten; Henry (H. S. Joyce), who was eight; Ellen (six); Dora (five); Janet (two), and six-month-old Thomas, who was born at Wimborne. Three employees are also listed – governess Annie Ball, aged 21; general servant Maria Swyers, aged 17; and nurse Susan Witcomb (18).

Armed with these basic facts, plus a photocopy of one of Joyce's books, I featured him in my Heritage column in the Bournemouth Evening Echo on February 24, 1994, together with the statement that no-one had yet discovered where he had lived after leaving Wimborne or where and when he had died. Enter Carole Parsons, who rang me after reading the article to say that she had not only known H. S. Joyce when she was a child but had always called him 'Grandad'. 'I was like an adopted daughter of the Joyce family,' she said, adding that they lived in north Devon, where she was brought up. It was a complete coincidence that Carole now found herself living at Colehill, Wimborne, and a further coincidence that she had happened to read the Evening Echo on that day, since she rarely bought the paper.

Carole put me in touch with H. S. Joyce's son and daughter-in-law Peter and Jean Joyce, who live near Barnstaple and were able to provide the many missing pieces of the jigsaw. 'My father – who was known in the family as "Harry" but to almost everyone else as "H. S." – was born at White Mill in 1882, went to Wimborne Grammar School and lived in his later childhood at Oaklands in Rowlands Hill,' said Peter. 'The family rented Cowgrove as a farm and Father was set to follow in his father's footsteps. But old Granny Joyce [Ellen senior] was a tyrant and ran the family with a rod of iron. Farming wasn't good enough for poor Harry, who was put into the National Provincial Bank at Poole. That was ludicrous – a wicked thing, because he had no interest whatsoever in banking. He was a countryman, a rural eccentric and a very observant naturalist. But he stayed with the bank until he retired.'

H. S.'s banking career soon took him away from Dorset. He was posted successively to Exeter, Beckenham, Plymouth, Dulverton, Swindon and eventually to Ashburton in Devon, where he was the branch manager until his retirement in 1938. He died in 1961. Ironically, H. S.'s banking commitments may have cost him what might otherwise have been the zenith of his second career as a writer-naturalist. According to his son, he was short-listed as the official naturalist for one of Sir Ernest Shackleton's expeditions to the Antarctic but the National Provincial Bank refused to release him. Peter's sister Jenny Down has a different version of this particular episode. 'Harry was in the same lodging house in Plymouth as Lawrence Oates and was fascinated by the plans for Scott's expedition,' she says. 'Oates wrote to Scott suggesting Harry as artist-naturalist but Scott wrote back saying that unfortunately the suggestion had come just too late as he had engaged someone for the position. Oates gave him Scott's letter, which I have read.' Given that Peter has Shackleton's signature on the official notepaper of the Imperial Trans-Antarctic Expedition, it is possible that both versions are true and that, having had his appetite whetted by Oates, H. S. approached Shackleton regarding a later expedition.

H. S. Joyce used to describe himself as 'the world's worst bank manager', but Peter said: 'He was a very successful bank manager – but he hated it! His banking career was solely to provide income for his family and the necessities of life and he took a particular pride in the fact that his painting and writing provided money for fishing, shooting and all his sporting activities.'

There seems to have been no end to H. S.'s talents – he was also a competent swimmer and lifesaving examiner (before the First World War he was lifesaving instructor to Plymouth Police) and a fine singer who performed in operatic productions and with the Barnstaple Male Voice Choir. His daughter has a fond memory of an occasion when the two of them were returning from rehearsals for a choral performance of *The Messiah*. 'We cycled home late at night with the music still ringing in our ears. Suddenly Harry burst into the Hallelujah Chorus. I joined in and together we pedalled our way home belting out that wonderful song at the tops of our voices. That was his "eccentricity", if you can call it that: his sheer exuberance and enthusiasm for life.'

More than anything, H. S. excelled as an eccentric and as a local character. 'He wore a tweed hat decorated with fishing flies and many darns, brown breeches which he darned himself, a darned jacket and thick shooting stockings which he also darned,' said Jean. 'The hat looked as if it had been run over several times or that he had cleaned his bike with it. He rode the biggest, oldest push-bike in the world – an old sit-up-and-beg bicycle with a wicker basket. He rode in the middle of the road,

White Mill in H.S. Joyce's childhood

paying no attention to the traffic round about and raising his hat to the ladies on the pavement. He always acknowledged the ladies! He was such a lovable person.'

Jenny recalls an occasion when her father was attempting to sew leather patches, 'country fashion', on the elbows of his fishing jacket, hampered by the family cat curled up on his lap.

'You don't think it would be simpler to buy a new jacket,' suggested his wife Elizabeth (nee Sanders).

'There is no disgrace in wearing clean patched clothes,' H. S. replied. 'The shame is when the clothes are neither.'

When Peter and Jean became engaged, Elizabeth took her future daughter-in-law to the refrigerator and told her: 'I must warn you – don't be surprised at anything you see.' Jean recalls: 'There were boxes, any of which might contain a bird's head, a skull, worms or insects!'

H. S. Joyce's seven books included *I Was Born in the Country*, a lively account of his childhood in Victorian Sturminster Marshall and Wimborne. The present volume includes the complete text of *I Was Born in the Country*, which was originally published by Art and Education Publishers in 1946; this volume also features articles on White Mill Bridge, Sturminster Marshall, and the nearby Iron Age hillfort of Badbury Rings, both taken from a collection of magazine articles which

White Mill today

appeared in book form as *By Field and Stream* (Borough Press, Swindon, 1934), and on Eyebridge at Cowgrove, which appeared in the *Dorset County Journal* in October-December 1948. Harry's other books were *Holiday Trout Fishing* (c1945), *A Trout Angler's Notebook* (c1948), *A Countryman's Notebook* (c1949), *Holidays With A Rod* (c1950) and *An Introduction to Coarse Fishing* (1952).

H. S. Joyce wrote for many of the leading magazines of his day, including *The Field, Country Life, Angling, The Boys' Own Paper, Field Sports, Wildlife, The Country Sportsman, The Nature Lover, The Fishing Gazette, Game and Gun* and *The Shooting Times*. For many years Peter Joyce's Christmas present from his father was the *Young England Annual*, which invariably contained an article by his father. H. S. was a regular broadcaster for the BBC and an artist who exhibited oils, watercolours and pen and ink drawings in London and several Devon towns. He illustrated his own books and articles.

Given the breadth of H. S.'s talents and the extent of his achievements as a writer, artist and broadcaster, it is quite amazing that until recently hardly anyone in Dorset had heard of him, apart from a few enthusiastic anglers who had been brought up with his books. One of the reasons for this is that, although brought up in East Dorset, H. S. left his native county in early adulthood, before he had had the opportunity to establish himself on the creative front; he did in fact become a well-known local character in north Devon, where he spent the later part of his life. Another reason is that in *I Was Born in the Country*, the only book devoted exclusively to Dorset, his identification of locations is curiously cryptic: Wimborne and Blandford are mentioned by name only once each (being otherwise referred to as 'the market towns'), while the names of Sturminster Marshall and Shapwick, the main parishes featured in the text, are not given at all (being referred to as 'the villages').

Hopefully this volume will help to elevate H. S. Joyce to his rightful place as one of Dorset's more notable worthies and the best of his Dorset writings to their due status as an important addition to the shelves of Dorset book collectors. Joyce was a great observer of everything around him and the book provides a unique window on to East Dorset in the late Victorian period and especially on to the wildlife of the time and village and rural life generally. It's a way of life that will already be familiar to many readers through the novels, short stories and poems of Dorset's greatest literary figure, Thomas Hardy. Reading, for example, Joyce's description in Chapter VI of the entire community pitching in to bring in the harvest, it is hard not to be reminded of certain scenes from Hardy. As I discovered by accident, it is an interesting experience to read *A Country Childhood* and a Hardy novel in tandem.

In editing this book, very few changes have been made to Joyce's original text (the handful of exceptions being minor alterations to grammar or punctuation) but a small number of footnotes have been added where appropriate in order to illuminate specific references. In a few instances H. S. Joyce uses a word or phrase that would have been totally acceptable in his time but may be politically incorrect today. In the interests of historical accuracy and the need to retain the flavour of the work, the author's original version has in each case been adhered to, with the addition of a footnote where appropriate.

On the subject of political correctness, it ought also to be mentioned that since H. S. Joyce's time there has been an enormous shift in public attitudes to various country activities. In his childhood (and even in his adulthood) hunting and shooting wild birds and animals and collecting birds' eggs were integral parts of the rural way of life, almost universally accepted by country people and rarely questioned even in the towns. Unlike many today, Joyce and his generation saw no conflict between these traditional country pursuits and a general love and interest in wildlife and the countryside. If H. S. is to be judged at all, he should therefore be judged in the context of his era and not by the standards of today. In fact, as his writings make clear, he exercised more selectivity and restraint in country sports than many of his generation, and adhered to the codes of conduct which the country people applied to these activities.

Those wishing to visit H. S. Joyce's birthplace, White Mill at Sturminster Marshall, will be interested to note that it is open to the public at weekends from Easter to October or by appointment with the National Trust's custodial tenant, Colin Cope.

It remains only to thank those who have assisted in various ways in the publication of this book, in particular Mark Bedford, the staff and volunteers of the National Trust at Kingston Lacy and the Priest's House Museum at Wimborne, Carole Parsons, Colin Cope, Bill Coomer and, most of all, Peter and Jean Joyce and Peter's sister Jenny Down, who have co-operated in every way.

R.G.

Water Rails

Chapter I

First Impressions

UNT Hayter, who was my father's aunt and therefore my great aunt, lived to be nearly a hundred. Towards the close of her life she developed a remarkable memory for incidents of her early childhood. She would sing songs, recite poetry and recount things that had happened when she was a mere baby at her mother's knee. This may be the usual thing in extreme old age and perhaps it is because I am not yet old enough that I have only a very hazy recollection of the events of my very early childhood. About the earliest incident that I have any clear memory of is that of sitting upon this old lady's knee, pushing my finger into her toothless mouth and then, after carefully feeling all around her gums for any sign of a bony protuberance, proudly exposing my own gums for her examination of the minute ivory points that were beginning to show and informing her that I was growing 'toofs more quicker' than she was.

Perhaps the next incident was a painful experience I suffered through the stupidity of a village girl we had as a nursemaid. This girl, with a view to impressing us with her cleverness, pretended to insert a small pebble into her nostril and withdrew it from her ear. I endeavoured to do the same, with the result that the pebble stuck and had to be extracted by my mother by the aid of a button hook. I howled with pain during this operation and was severely slapped by my mother for doing so; her violence being no doubt caused by her extreme agitation.

Then follow several recollections connected with the maids. A terrifying experience with a bull; that frequently repeated itself in frightful nightmares and the evidence of which still remains (or did remain but a few years ago) in a bent rail against the further slope of the bridge. Our nurse was taking my sister and myself for an airing along the straight level road that led to the village. I was in the 'pram'; my sister was walking alongside wearing a little red cape. I suppose it was the colour of the cape that annoyed the bull. At any rate I suddenly found myself bouncing along the road in my chariot, with the maid pushing and screaming, and dragging my terrified sister at her heels. Across the meadows came tearing a great white bull; at least, my recollection of it is that it was white, though I think it more likely that its colour was a light roan, since that was the popular colour for bulls in those parts and pure white such a rarity that I do not believe I have ever seen one. The bull came rushing down upon us and leapt at the rails bordering the road. Then fate decided that we should not be hurled over the parapet into the river. One the creature's feet caught in the rails; there was a loud snap and the animal fell into the road with one of its legs broken. That was the last I saw of it; but I suppose someone came along later and put it out of its misery. But the heavy pipe railing, more than an inch in diameter, was bent and no one bothered to straighten it.

On another occasion, a few years later, we were taking a walk down 'Jig-Jog' lane, a pretty green track about half a mile from home which was thus named by us on account of the deep ruts made by the farm carts and the curiously regular ridges made by the hooves of sheep each treading in each other's footsteps. Our nurse pointed out to me a large hole in the bank and declared it was a fox's hole. I peeped in and, noticing that there was a very powerful scent, declared that there must be a fox inside and that I would push it out with my whip. This whip was a leather thing with a black wooden whistle fixed in the end of the handle; I had received it as a Christmas present and could never be persuaded to go for a walk without it. I thrust the whip down the hole; then suddenly took fright at the thought of the possibility of Reynard jumping out in my face. The whip slipped from my hand and disappeared down the hole. Of course there was a tremendous hullaballoo, which continued even after I had reached home. Fortunately the cook had a sweetheart, one known to us as 'the pretty man' because of his bright blue eyes and curly hair, whose daily work took him past the lane. On hearing of my misfortune, she promised that she would get her young man to recover the whip for me, which he did the next day, much to my joy. I don't know if 'the pretty man' ever married the cook; but, if he did, I think it probable that she made him very happy, for she was really a very fine woman. She was always kind to us children; much kinder than we deserved, I expect; for I am sure we must often have been a sore trial to her. One of the chief things I remember about her was her affection for the cats which swarmed about the place. There were always at least a dozen and on wet days at least half the tribe would be found seated around the kitchen fire. The cats were kept because of the rats and mice which infested the mill and a room which gave free access to the mill buildings was set apart for their use. During the winter, floods were common and were sometimes so deep and of such long duration that we were cut off from the rest of the world for several days, and a horse and wagon had to be put at the disposal of the workmen to fetch them to work and return to their homes in the village across the river at the end of the day. It was during a particularly severe flood that cook was awakened one night by the piteous mewing of her beloved cats. She lit her candle and went downstairs. To get to the cats' room she had to pass along a little glass-roofed passage which she now found a foot deep in water. She hoisted her nightgown and stepped into the cold, muddy flood. The cats' room was at a lower level than the passage and, on reaching the door and opening it she saw her pets seated in a bunch on a table and yowling for all they were worth. The table careered swiftly round the room, carried along by a great eddy and bumping against the walls as it twirled and rocked on its course. Cook watched her opportunity and grabbed one of the cats as the table passed the doorway. Then she waded back along the passage and deposited the frightened creature on the hearthrug in the kitchen. It took her over an hour to rescue all those cats and then she first made up the fire for their further comfort before herself retiring to warm her own legs for an hour beneath the bedclothes before she again rose to carry out her usual daily duties.

It must have been about this period of my existence that 'Mumming'[1] was a favourite winter occupation of the village men. I have only a very hazy recollection of the Mummers performance. The men, some of whom I recognised, painted their faces stuck feathers in their hats, and tied ribbons to their clothes. One, at any rate, had a concertina; there was also a doctor, a Turk and St. George. They came into the kitchen, danced about in a grotesque fashion, did some sort of a play in which the doctor, the Turk and St. George had prominent parts, and received a bread and cheese meal and some money.

Of the farm work itself I saw nothing until I was about five or six years old. I saw the horses go out to work and come back again in the evening and I knew some of them by name. When Venture's dead body passed the house, I saw a tear roll down Father's cheek. I went away and hid myself and wept bitterly. That was the first time my Father's grief was mine; but ever after that every sign of sorrow in his face was a source of grief to me, and many days I went away by myself to cry because I knew that some trouble had fallen upon him.

---

1 Mummers' plays were a popular Christmas tradition in England until the early 20th century.

The fowls, ducks, pigeons and pigs, were always in view from the windows. In those days they were all white, in keeping with the name of the place – 'White Mill'. Mother's little fantails were a constant source of amusement as they strutted about with their heads touching their upturned tails. The ducks were good-natured creatures and looked up sideways with a knowing, comical expression when we called 'dilly, dilly' and threw out food for them, but the fowls were stupid and quarrelsome. The cocks were always fighting and during one terrible period even the hens became afflicted with the same quarrelsomeness and fought dreadful battles. I remember seeing one poor, blinded bird plunge its head into the garden hedge with its eyes hanging from their sockets. We all cried bitterly till someone came and took the poor 'coopie' away, no doubt to put an end to its sufferings. The pigeons soon became mixed in colour by reason of their periodical migration to the next farm, about half a mile away. The tenant of this farm was a widow and she employed a bailiff to manage it for her. From time to time, in order to reduce the number of birds, Father would invite the bailiff over to help him shoot some of the pigeons. Many of the survivors would then desert our roof and join up with the mixed pigeons at the other farm; returning again later on, and bringing others with them, when an exchange visit was paid to shoot off the surplus at the other place.

On Sundays we were sometimes taken to the church in the village across the river. I can remember two things only in connection with those visits; one was an occasion when I was very severely slapped for calling attention to a Red Admiral butterfly that was fluttering up and down one of the windows, and the other was the parson's curious habit of going on and on in the prayers, completely ignoring all marks of punctuation, until he ran out of breath; then pausing, in the middle of a sentence if necessary, and continuing in the same manner when he had replenished his bellows. More than thirty years later I attended the funeral of a friend at that church. The old parson[2] conducted the service and he still ignored all stops and commas and only halted when he was compelled to for want of breath.

We had a good many visitors for a family living more than four miles from a town. Father had a remarkably fine singing voice and Mother also was extremely fond of music. This brought them into touch with a great many interesting people. Many artists also came to paint the mill and its surroundings and all were welcomed to our meals if they would.

---

2 The Rev. James Cross was Vicar of Sturminster Marshall from 1877-1931.

FIRST IMPRESSIONS

About Christmas time Mother always gave a children's party. At one of these gatherings Father and a friend of his gave us a magic lantern show on a sheet stretched across the door of the dining room. One slide showed a man asleep with his mouth open and down his mouth ran scores of mice. This was encored again and again; although I believe it was supposed to be one of those hated things, a story with a moral; the moral being 'don't sleep with your mouth open.'

One day we were told we were to have visitors from Australia, where the black people lived. We were all agog to see these strangers, for we had never seen a live black person. Presently a gig drove up containing a man and woman, and a little boy. As they were all the same colour as ourselves, we did not take very great interest in them, until our nurse came into the nursery and announced 'They be come.' We were taken down and presented and were very disappointed to find that these indeed were the Australians. The little boy, however, gave us some amusement at tea by removing all the caraway seeds from his cake and placing them round the edge of his plate. When his mother remonstrated with him for his bad manners, he replied, 'But I don't like fleas in my cake.'

Sometimes big men arrived with heavy clothes, rods and bags. They would disappear for the day and return later to tea, bringing with them gigantic pike with frightful jaws that snapped viciously as the fish were laid on the cold stones in the scullery. It is rather curious to note that, though our river swarmed with fish and our garden and the lanes were full of birds, I have no recollection of seeing a live fish until I was about eight years old, or of noticing any wild birds other than robins, blackbirds, thrushes and sparrows. Later on fish and birds were to become to me the most absorbing of all the things to be seen about the farm and river.

To keep me in order, Father sometimes tanned me with a little hazel stick which was always kept in view behind a small water colour painting of the mill. The threat of having 'Tommy Tickle-mouse' brought to me was often sufficient to reduce me to a reasonable state of mind when I flew into one of my frequent and violent fits of temper; but I can only remember one of the many occasions on which it was applied and that was the last. I was in a particularly violent mood and was kicking and screaming, and completely out of control. Father was called and, having failed in his efforts to subdue me by appeals and threats, took down the stick and put me across his knees. I think he had probably lost all patience with me and hit me much harder than he had intended. The stick broke. A moment before I had been kicking and yelling whilst I was being held in position to receive the blow but the breaking of the stick quieted me at once. It also caused Father to regain his composure. 'There now! Perhaps that will be a lesson to you,' he said as he put me down; 'And you try and be a better boy in future.' I was completely subdued by this astonishing event: he had broken the stick – across the heel of my boot and didn't know it! I have since learnt what a shock it can be to a parent to think that he has unduly hurt one of his own children.

Mother had a pony and buggy, and in this we sometimes went with her when she drove to take tea with some of her friends. I suppose we visited all the farmhouses within easy driving distance; but I can remember only two as places visited during my early childhood. In one, two great stuffed swans stood in glass cases in the hall and, though I could see a live swan almost any day on the river, these birds looked so enormous that they made a tremendous impression on me. In the other it was a picture that attracted my attention, a coloured reproduction of the famous painting 'Shoeing the Bay Mare.' This was the first picture I can remember as having really noticed. It became my chief interest whenever I went to that house and still remains one of my great favourites.

I remember two other incidents in connection with this last house. In one case the lady was demonstrating to my Mother the advantages of a self-pouring teapot that had recently arrived. All one had to do was to put the cup under the spout, press the lid, and the tea gushed out. For the sake of symmetry in design, I suppose, the handle and the spout looked very much alike, each being curved over to exactly the same length. Unfortunately the cup had been placed beneath the wrong curve and, as the lady turned to my Mother to remark on the simplicity of the device, my eyes nearly popped out of my head with delight at seeing the tea spreading in a flood all over the tray.

Another odd incident at the same house has stuck in my memory. The lady had friends from abroad staying with her and they had brought with them their servant who was a native of the country in which they had been living. After tea, this girl was brought into the drawing room and gave us a demonstration of her native shawl dance. She pranced and capered about the room with a great length of green muslin waving around her. It may have been very clever and very artistic; to me it appeared rather ridiculous. At any rate it was certainly an unusual performance to witness in a late Victorian drawing room in a farmhouse.

About this time I met with a painful and rather curious accident. In the wall of the nursery was a headless nail. I was playing with one of my sisters with a large coloured rubber ball and was standing right against the wall in which was this nail. The ball hit me in the face, and I bobbed my head back onto the nail and stuck fast. I don't remember if I pulled myself off, or if someone came to my rescue; but I retained a small bald spot at the back of my head as a memento of the occasion right into my adult life. Another accident taught me that cats could scratch and also taught me to be kind to animals. Tommy, the favourite old grey tom cat, had annoyed me about something, so I threw him downstairs. He immediately sprang back, swiped me across the face with his claws and bolted. I was left with a rather badly cut lip and a resolve not to be rough with the cats in future.

I have seen many farm houses and mills since those days and no doubt many of them have been more beautiful and with far greater comforts than were to be found about the old building which stands on the banks of the old Dorsetshire Stour halfway between Wimborne and Blandford; and I daresay I have seen far lovelier and grander rivers than that rather slowly moving stream: but no farm, mill, or river has ever really taken their place. To me they will always be 'home;' just as they remained 'home' to Father all his days. Some people seem to be born without roots; it matters little to them where they have to live, provided they can have what they consider essential comforts. Others always suffer at each transplantation. The roots of their lives seem to spread so widely and deeply that some are broken off and, if they are some of their tenderest, early roots, they seem to leave a lasting mark; a wound that may heal, but which will always carry a scar. I think I am one of this sort.

The Kingfisher

Chapter II
Becoming a Boy

AVING attained the dignity of being 'breeched,' I began to feel a great deal more confidence in myself; an early indication of the effect clothing has upon the wearer. I began to feel a boy and adopted a more self-assertive attitude towards many things My nurse soon found that I had a will of my own and I received a good many vigorous tugs and slaps when my stubbornness obstructed her in her duties towards me. My budding confidence enabled me to face the dangers of the road alone. I did not go far, but I reached the mill and the bakehouse and smelt the dusty, sweet smell of the former and the rich, warm smell of the latter. Smelling is a very primitive sense and was undoubtedly at one period of our history a very valuable asset. Early smells probably contribute far more than we imagine to the make-up of our adult lives. The smells that I like best of all are those connected with my earliest days. Many are definitely repugnant to the majority of people. I delight in the smell of horses and cows, sheep folded on roots, pigs in sties - not the sour smell of farmyard manure; but the somewhat sweet scent that comes from clean pigs fattening on fresh barley meal. Freshly ground corn, new-baked bread, freshly-turned earth, hay, wood fires, field couch fires, rushes, apples and the smell of black shag tobacco smoked out of doors on a frosty morning, all give me great pleasure. The next definite sense to be awakened seems to have been the sense of hearing. I began to notice not only the difference between human voices, but the sounds connected with definite places or objects. The swish of a scythe, the hum of a threshing machine, the rumble of a wagon, milk falling in regular jets into a pail, the early morning talk of ducks and fowls, the confused babel of bleating from a large flock of sheep, the cries of water birds, the creak of a plough, the rattle of a horse-roller, the double note of a pump handle and the squealing of pigs at feeding time. These sounds still stir me and give me a strange feeling of contentment.

My journeys to the mill and bakehouse were never allowed to extend further in that direction; as beyond the latter lay the river and therein lay great danger to a small, venturesome child. I could cross the road to the garden as often as I wished, for there I was in sight from the house and well-protected all round by a sound fence. The garden was supposed to be quite safe, though a minor danger was hidden in a clump of pampas grass; but, after cutting my hands rather badly on the sharp-edged blades of this plant, I soon learned to avoid it. I also learnt that hens that had 'stolen' their nests in the shrubberies could inflict very painful pecks when interfered with. The garden was really a very beautiful spot and, because it was divided into several parts, appeared much more extensive than was really the case. The first, or lower part, consisted of two small lawns, some rookeries and clover beds, the clump of pampas grass, and some box shrubberies. Then came a steep bank, clothed with lime trees and traversed diagonally by a sloping path and two short flights of stone- steps. At the top of the steps was a little summer house looking on to a small lawn shielded by a high hornbeam hedge; and, beyond that again, the vegetable plots and fruit trees, with a path down the middle which ended in a stile leading into a grass field. Another method of reaching this elevated part of the garden was by a sloping path through a grove of horse chestnut and other trees. In the spring time the sloping bank and the ground beneath the trees was spotted white and yellow with the blooms of hundreds of snowdrops and daffodils. Playing in the garden was usually a quiet, peaceable occupation; making daisy chains, having tea on the lawn, or playing with a ball. From time to time exciting diversion would be caused by the entry of a tribe of small pigs from the yard. It was then my great delight to send one of my sisters to hold the yard gate open whilst I herded the pigs out of the garden and into their rightful domain. This was a by-no-means easy task, for even very small pigs invariably prefer to go in a direction exactly opposite to that which it is your wish they should go.

We did not see much of Father except for a short time after tea and before we were packed off to bed. He would then sit back in his arm chair with one leg crossed over the knee of the other. I could never resist this raised foot and would struggle on to it as soon as possible for a ride. Father would then recite the following lines:

> 'This is the way the ladies ride;
> Trot-at-a-trot, trot-at-a-trot.
> This is the way the gentlemen ride;
> Gallop-a-trot, gallop-a-trot.
> This is the way the farmers ride:
> Jiggety-jog, jiggety-jog.'

BECOMING A BOY

The action of the leg suited the words and at the last line became so vigorous that, though I clung on by hands and knees, I very soon rolled off
on to the floor. But soon I was getting too heavy for this sort of thing and,
when I scrambled up in the hopes of a game, Father would excuse himself
by saying that he had a bone in his leg. This was said as if it was some
painful complaint he was suffering from and it was a very long time before
I saw through this trick. But I had to be amused in some way and he would
give me a piece of paper and a pencil and get me to copy one of several
little drawings he made for me: a duck in one continuous line; a mouse or
a pig - just ovals with a point at one end and a wavy or twisty line at the
other, and four strokes for legs; the difference between the two animals
consisting chiefly in that the mouse had round ears, whiskers and a long
tail, whilst the pig had a blunt end to its nose, no whiskers, pointed ears
and a very short tail. These early drawing lessons sowed the seeds of a
hobby that has lasted me all my life and given me more pleasure than anything else I have ever learnt.

About this time I had my first real lesson in manners. 'Company' and
'Table' manners were a natural part of our upbringing and I think we were
fairly well grounded in them. But I was now to learn something deeper
and more sincere than these things. My sisters and I were in the nursery
one day and I was seated before the open window. Few people passed that
way and those who did were mostly well-known to us; so that we would
usually, look out on hearing passing footsteps and perhaps call a greeting
if the passer should happen to be someone we knew. A man came down
the road and turned round the corner of the house towards the mill. He
was a ragged-looking individual with a long red beard and, on his back,
suspended from his shoulders by a piece of string, hung a square withy
basket. 'Who is that?' asked one of my sisters who was seated on the floor
and therefore could not see down into the road. 'Only some old tramp.' I
replied. A few minutes later a message came that Dad wished to see me in
the bakehouse. I went down and found my Father and the ragged man
standing before the oven. 'What did you say this man was?' asked Father.
'I said he was only an old tramp' I replied, blushing crimson. 'Well, he is
not a tramp' said Dad. 'He is an honest watercress seller and a friend of
mine. You must tell him that you are sorry for what you said and promise
that you will never be rude to him again.'

Of course I did as I was told, and of course I felt very guilty and foolish. 'Now run along indoors and be a good boy' said Father. I was glad to
get away; but when I regained the nursery I was too ashamed to tell my

sisters what had happened. I never forgot this lesson: that an honest man, no matter what his state of life or fortune, is worthy of respect. One result of this is that I have made a great many friendships with people in all sorts of positions in life and have found plenty of good everywhere. Father had friends in every walk of life. He loved all honest men and did not bother about their stations or callings. He hated to hear evil of any-one and, if ever I repeated something I had heard to someone's disadvantage, he would say 'You shouldn't listen to such talk.' Amongst his friends was a charming little old nigger[3] who went about the country breaking chains on his biceps, doing acrobatic feats and 'fire-eating.' When driving, Father would never pass this little man without stopping to give him a lift and in return the nigger[3] would tell of his travels and of the careful, hard life he was obliged to live in order to keep himself fit for his performance. I think he must have been nearly seventy years old when I first met him; yet he stood upright and vigorous, and walked with a springy step. His thick, kinky hair was almost pure white and, when he smiled, his face became really beautiful. When I read Uncle Tom's Cabin some years later, I pictured the hero of that story as just such another as Father's little black friend.

I had not yet reached that stage of a boy's existence when girls were 'only girls.' I did not, therefore, object to sharing the same large bed with my eldest sister. My second sister was almost a cripple and so slept in another room with the nurse. Perhaps Dora, the baby, was also in that room; but I cannot remember. My eldest sister proved a very good companion and we invented several interesting games to pass away any wakeful periods. We were always given a sweet each when retiring to bed and, when these happened to be 'ju-jubes,' we could suck off all the sugar and then, pursing our lips, shoot the remaining blob of jelly into space. If the sweet was found upon the floor next day it was recovered and eaten, a healthy morning appetite removing any squeamishness we might have felt concerning whose mouth it might have been in on the previous evening. But many of these ju-jube cores hit the walls and disappeared. When spring cleaning was in progress, a row of dust-covered balls of jelly were discovered lodged behind every picture in the room and I received due reprimand for our ' disgusting behaviour.' Another delightful game was gnat killing. Gnats were very plentiful during the summer. They bred in the

---

3 In Joyce's time the word 'nigger' was in common usage and did not have the racial overtones that it does today.

muddy pools by the river and also in the water butt that stood outside the back door. We used to stand on a stool and look down into the clear water in the butt to watch the 'wrigglers' as we called the gnat larvae, kicking their way up to the surface for air and sinking down again into the depths. The adult gnats often entered the bedroom windows and in the dusk they would come humming across the room. We hated the gnats because of the painful bites they inflicted on us; so we would wait clutching the sheet until the sound came quite close to our faces. 'Now!' one of us would exclaim. Then down would come the top of the sheet and we would 'iron' it out with all our might with the palms of our hands. Next morning we would turn back the top of the sheet and search for the flattened corpse of our victim. Mother often put a branch of elder at the head of the bed to keep the gnats away; the carter also put elder branches on the heads of his horses for the same purpose.

Often on a winter's evening Mother's small drawing-room became almost uncomfortably full of musical friends. We children were not allowed to sit up; but we could leave the bedroom door open so that we could hear the songs and playing. Father never sang 'trash' as he called it and I can never remember learning any but worth-while songs sung in our house. Father's favourites were ballads and the various solo items from oratorios. Such as 'To Anthea,' 'A Warrior Bold,' 'To Julia,' 'O'er Normandy's Blue Hills' were great favourites of his and he sang them as I have never heard them sung by anyone else. Artists with the brush, also, were frequent visitors. The mill and the bridge were favourite scenes and must have formed the subjects of many scores of pictures. Though Father was no painter, his naturally artistic temperament placed him at once on a good footing with those who came to paint and he made many friends amongst them. There were also the pike fishers. They usually arrived soon after breakfast in a horse conveyance and, after stabling their horse, would come stamping indoors in their heavy boots and leggings to greet Mother before setting out for the day beside the river. At that time I knew nothing of what they did; but I was always eager to see the fish laid out on the scullery floor when they returned at night.

The first bird's nest that I remember seeing was that of a robin. It was pointed out to me by the nursemaid and, when I stretched out my hand to touch the eggs within, she hastily stopped me and told me that if ever I touched a robin's egg I should have a crooked finger. I never forgot the warning and I must have seen dozens of robin's nests before I dared at length defy the saying and take one of the eggs. Another curious saying that

Coal tit and marsh tit

took a very strong hold of me was that nettles 'didn't sting this month.' It took me a good many years to get at the real meaning of these statements.

Nowadays one may often see a young farm labourer going to work on a motor cycle. When I was a small boy those who did not walk to work came on 'penny-farthings.' I have never attempted to mount one of these extraordinary machines and I have always regarded doing so, particularly when carrying across one's back a rush basket containing a good supply of food and drink, an acrobatic feat of no mean order. Sometimes the rider had to make several attempts before he could get astride his machine, hop-hop-hopping, down the road with one foot on the step and the bicycle wobbling along in front of him. The learning must have required consid-erable courage and determination. I learnt to ride a donkey and that was a very nerve-racking business; but the animal could at least stand up on its legs without requiring any assistance from me in balancing.

That donkey gave us all a great deal of pleasure and enabled us to travel a great deal further from home than we could do without its assistance. We even got as far as the downs, one riding on a certain distance and waiting there until the rest of the party caught up: then dismounting and letting someone else get into the saddle, who would then trot away a further quarter mile on the road. Father told me that he even rode hunting on a donkey when he was a small boy; but we never attempted such an adventure as that. Our donkey was eventually sold and was turned out in an orchard for its first night in its new home. In this orchard was a swing. Next morning the donkey was found dead with its head in the swing, which was twisted up so that the poor animal's forequarters were right off the ground. We wept when we heard of this tragedy and declared that poor Neddy had committed suicide because he was so unhappy at leaving us. I imagine that the donkey rested its head on the seat of the swing. Perhaps a change in the wind during the night caused it to shift its position slightly so as to get the wind behind it, as animals generally do. This movement would cause the ropes to cross and thus restrict the movement of the animal's head, perhaps even prevent its withdrawal. Its efforts to escape would naturally cause it to move in a circle and, not having sufficient intelligence to reverse the process, each step would tighten the ropes about it, until finally its forefeet would be lifted from the ground and strangulation would then be only be a matter of time. I do not think that our romantic translation of the incident had any relation to the truth.

The possession of a pocket knife is a definite landmark in the life of every boy. At length one came for me in a Christmas hamper. Of course I was warned not to cut myself and of course I did. George took a great interest in it when I proudly showed it to him and he soon taught me how to make popguns and whistles out of elder sticks: he also showed me how to make a pipe by hollowing out an acorn and inserting a piece of dead dock as a stem. This was rather unwise of him, because I was not content with having the pipe: but had to experiment with smoking. The nearest approach to tobacco that I could find was the dead heads of clover flowers. I collected some of these, pressed them into the bowl, sneaked a box of matches from the kitchen mantlepiece and retired to the seclusion of the garden closet. This place was situated behind the shrubberies and beyond the box arbour in the lower garden. It was a family affair and contained three seats, two for adults and one little one in the centre for a child. It backed on to the yard and the cess pit was ingeniously arranged so that it could be cleaned out from the yard when the yard dung was being removed. I don't know why many of these old fashioned places were made with three seats, as I never knew them to be used by more than one person at a time. I sat there and smoked my pipe and felt very much the man. Then I began to feel ill. I retired to the box arbour and bravely continued smoking. I began to feel worse; so I thought I would try and find Father. I really thought I was going to die. I staggered out of the garden and started up the road; but I didn't get far. A dreadful giddiness overcame me and I collapsed into the hedge. Just then the squire came driving by in his carriage and pair. He saw Father in the field beyond and sent his coachman to tell him that I was lying ill in the ditch. I don't remember anything more about this adventure but I know that I never told anyone the reason for my sickness.

I had a white rabbit given to me and this was kept in a hutch at the back of the summer house. I was allowed to help myself to bran for it and for green food I collected cow parsley from beneath the trees on the slope leading up to the summer house. This slope had two crops of flowers each year. The first was a fine show of bluebells and later on the cow parsley came into flower and covered the ground with a mass of filmy white blossoms.

Another present gained me the name of 'Cap'n.' It was in the form of four little boats with sails attached to two strips of wood and fixed on the top of a pole. Old Uncle Hayter made it for me and it was set up just inside the garden gate. On a windy day the little boats raced round after each other at a terrific rate.

I had often seen the men about the place throw stones and knock over rabbits; so of course I had to try my hand at this game. At first I met with disaster and broke a few windows, for which I got a tanning. Then two more serious incidents occurred which made me realise the danger of the practice. In one I threw a stone at the ducks to make them jump into the pond in the chalk pit and broke the wing of one of them. I told no one about this, but I was really very upset. I had no intention of hurting the duck and I was very sorry for what I had done. In the other, I hurled a stone up into the pear tree to knock down some fruit for one of my sisters. The stone bounced off a branch and pitched on her head. 'That hit me on the head' she said and stooped to pick up a pear that had been knocked down. Then her hat fell off and she saw a pool of blood inside. She at once let out a terrific scream and ran howling indoors to tell Mother that I had thrown a stone at her. I got a thrashing for this; but it took a long time for me to forgive this Eve-like meanness of my sister. I knew she could not have been really hurt, as it was not until she saw the blood in her hat that she started howling; and she said nothing about having asked me to knock down the pear, as she knew quite well that we were not allowed to help ourselves to fruit. I practised my stone-throwing more carefully after this and eventually became so proficient that, when I went to school, I was always given a position on the cricket field where I could knock down the wicket with a long throw. I knocked out three of our opponents in one match by this means. I killed a great many rabbits and rats with well-directed stones; but the only birds I ever threw at were sparrows. From quite an early age I took an interest in wild birds and, though I started an egg collection, I never went beyond two of any sort and was always particular to make quite sure that I knew the species of bird whose eggs I was taking. I spent two hours hidden in a bush waiting for a sight of the layer of my first coal tit's egg. I knew it was not a blue tit's and the only thing to do to make certain of the species was to lay up and identify the bird. The slap-dab way in which most of my school fellows collected eggs annoyed me very much and a Master who cut out and removed the whole of a clutch of kingfisher's eggs from a nest in one of our meadows so infuriated me that I refused to take off my hat to him, as we were supposed to do when meeting a Master outside the school, and always looked the other way and pretended not to have seen him.

Mallard landing

Chapter III
The River

HE river had always attracted me, but every time I went in its direction someone was sure to open a window and shout 'Don't you go down by that river, or you'll get drowned!' But at last I was allowed to go down with Father to be taken for a 'row in the boat.' This tremendous adventure consisted of sitting on the box at the end of a heavy rush-punt and being pushed about over the shallows by means of a long, iron-shod pole. It was a marvellous experience. The water was clear as crystal and Father pointed out to me the various fishes that inhabited this part of the river. There were shoals of minnows in the stiller water near the bank; fat-faced gudgeon digging in the gravel a little further out, and, where the water was about two or three feet deep, shoals of silvery dace that rushed upstream and down at our approach. There was even an eel living on the bottom in one place. Father put the end of the punt-pole near it and it at once darted off out of sight into a bed of weeds. From that time on I was always on the alert to take any opportunity of going in the boat. I also begged to be allowed to fish; for Father sometimes brought in a large pike or eel which he had taken on a night line.

My first fishing expedition was for gudgeon. Father rigged up some tackle on an old rod, dug some worms and took me out in the boat. He pushed off a few yards from the shore and lowered the 'anchor' which consisted of a couple of plough-shares attached to a chain. Next he scraped the bottom of the river with the end of the punt-pole until the water was thoroughly muddied, telling me that this was to attract the fish. Sure enough, no sooner had the cloud of disturbed mud floated away than a crowd of gudgeon could be seen nosing excitedly in the clear patch of gravel that had been uncovered. Father lowered his worm amongst them and in a second had a fat little fish kicking on the end of his line. He repeated this several times and then handed the rod to me. In a moment he called 'You've got one!' I saw the line move off, heaved quickly with the rod, felt some resistance for a second, and then the wormless hook flew over my head. I could not understand why I had failed to catch the fish and felt disappointed and impatient. 'Never mind,' said Father, 'Try again. You'll catch one next time.' I tried and lost several more worms before at last I felt something tremendously heavy kicking at the end of the line. I heaved with all my might and a fish came flying out of the water, whirled around my head, and wrapped the line about my neck. Father grabbed the fish quickly lest I should, in my excitement, get the hook into my hand. I was very proud of that fish, though it was barely five inches long. It seemed a whopper to me and I felt that I should soon be as good a fisherman as my cousins who sometimes caught perch from the bridge. When at length I really did go perch fishing, the second fish I captured that day was one of over two pounds and was almost the largest perch I have ever caught in my life.

Father taught me a great deal about the inhabitants of the river. He showed me the special places beloved of the perch: gravelly holes near bends or under trees, or against moss-covered posts driven in to protect the banks against the scouring of floods. Roach preferred the deeper parts and could be seen only when the water was very clear; though sometimes in the summer they could be seen swimming about near the surface in some quiet backwater. Pike always lived in the stillest water and one rarely saw very large ones; they remained deep down in the bends where water-lilies spread their broad leaves to shelter them. The big ones I saw brought in by the visitors in winter rather frightened me, especially when they gave a convulsive struggle and brought their terrible jaws together with a terrific snap. I felt that I should have to catch one of those great brutes one day; but I dreaded the time. Really the catching of my first pike was a very tame affair. Instructed by my Father, I had hooked a gudgeon to the tackle provided and heaved it out into the still waters of the hatch pool. Presently the float disappeared. I had been told to let the fish run and give it plenty of time to swallow the bait. I followed these instructions carefully and at length tightened up my line and struck. There was a terrific pull at the other end and the line rushed off towards some water-lilies. I saw the lilies waving about; but, though I pulled my hardest, I could not recover an inch of line. I put down the rod and ran off to look for Father. I found him in the bakehouse and he at once got out the boat and poled it up to the hatch pool. When we reached the lily bed, there was my pike caught up in the long stems of the plants. Father lifted it out, and replaced it in the water. 'Not worth keeping' he said. It was a little jack of about two pounds, and these fish, being the game fish of our river, were never retained unless they reached a weight of three or four pounds. I felt very disappointed at having no fish to show after all this fuss and excitement; but it was not long before I was able to drag a really sizeable pike out of the river and carry it proudly home, holding it, as I had been shown, by inserting a finger and thumb into its eye sockets.

Some time later I was introduced into the mysteries of spinning for pike by one of my cousins. He, having far more pocket money than I possessed, was provided with a Nottingham reel, special line, swivelled traces and artificial spinners. I was thrilled at the way in which he hurled his bait across the river and turning the handle of his reel brought it twinkling back to his feet. He caught a good many pike with his spinners and suggested that I should get the necessary tackle and also try. I felt almost ashamed to admit that my money consisted of a few coppers only, earned by doing odd jobs for father, and would never run to such an expensive outfit. Taking pity on me he presented me with a rubber wagtail. But, though I now had a spinning bait, I was in difficulty to know how I could use it; for my reel had no check that I could release and apply at will, and any attempt to cast with it merely resulted in the bait whirling around in the air and catching me a crack on the back of the head. But Father helped me out of my difficulty by showing me the way trollers (of which there were still a few in the district) cast their baits. In this method of fishing no reel is required; or at any rate it is not essential. The line, an ordinary twisted water cord, cheap but very strong, is allowed to trail on the ground. The right hand holds the rod and the left hand recovers the line, about a foot at a time, over the extended first finger of the right hand. One advantage of this method is that the grasses through which the line trails drag out most of the kinks, which, in the case of twisted water cord, begin to form almost as soon as one starts fishing.

I found this spinning a very interesting way of fishing; but it was some days before I caught a pike by this means. The fish would dash out from dark corners as the bait flashed by; but their appearance was so terrifying that my nerves would not stand up to the attack and I would whip the bait out of the water and over my head before the fish had time to grab it. This went on for some time, until I began to feel seriously distressed about it. I felt that I should never have courage enough to allow one of these fierce brutes to take hold of my bait. I happened to be fishing in 'Lower Ground,' a particularly quiet spot. Glancing around to see that no one was in sight, I retreated to a tree and, kneeling down, prayed fervently that I should be allowed to catch a fish. I then took up my rod again, feeling very full of courage, and heaved the bait to the far side of the river. I had not drawn in a couple of yards of line and the bait was still far out of sight, when I felt a heavy weight pulling against me. I immediately thought of weeds and felt that the Almighty was about to mock me by causing me to lose my precious bait at the very first throw after my prayer. But suddenly the rod top was bent down violently and the line was dragged through my fingers. I had hooked a pike! I don't know how long it took me, or how I got the fish on to the bank: but I got it ashore somehow and, taking it into the middle of the meadow, gave it a vigorous kick between the eyes to kill it before I attempted to remove the hooks. That pike weighed nearly six pounds and was the largest I had ever caught. I felt extraordinarily proud that I was thus able to provide a good meal for the whole family. From that time forward I caught quite a respectable number of pike with my wagtail bait, but I never quite got over my fear of them when they dashed out suddenly from under the bank and I know that from this cause alone I have missed almost as many as I have caught.

Perhaps it was a bathing incident that started my fear of pike. My cousins and I were strolling up the river one hot, sunny day and presently coming to a quiet spot overlooking a broad shallow, we sat down on the bank to rest. My cousins had their terrier with them and this dog lay down beside us and was soon fast asleep. Presently one of us suggested a bathe. We took off our clothes and prepared to enter the water. At that moment the terrier woke up. It gazed at us in wonder for a moment. It could not understand how we could have become suddenly and completely skinned. Its eyes grew in size and the hair of its back stood up on end. Then suddenly it leapt to its feet, gave one despairing howl, tucked in its tail and fled. We called and whistled; but that only made the dog run faster. Straight as an arrow it raced across the meadows, through the ditches and hedges, then across the cultivated fields, till at length we saw it dive through the garden hedge of my cousins' home nearly a mile away. When we had finished laughing, we clambered down the bank and into the river. The stream at this place was cut up into many channels by beds of waving, white flowered water ranunculus. Most of the channels were about three feet deep and so afforded safe and pleasant spots for us to splash about in. I was half-reclining in one of these channels, enjoying the cool sweep of the water along my body and the warmth of the sun on my head; my cousins being about ten yards above me. One of them, getting near the weeds, disturbed a pike, which raced out downstream. Hearing a shout, I stood up and at once saw the fish coming towards me. Before I could attempt to get out of the way, it had dashed into my legs and knocked them from under me, sending me right under water. As I had not yet learnt to swim, I was badly scared; I was also quite under the impression that the fish had deliberately attacked me. It was only after a considerable number of years had passed that I began to realise the possibility that the pike might have been fleeing in terror from my cousins and had bumped into me by accident. Even now I am sure I should have distinctly unpleasant feelings in my stomach if I happened to be swimming in a pool and knew that there was a big pike beneath me.

I very soon found that the river generally held more interest in one hundred yards than any sort of land could hold in half a mile. In the water itself were a great many varieties of fish. There were also many sorts of legged things in the water, by far the largest of which were the crayfish, or freshwater lobsters. In the summer months flies of many sorts danced and flitted above the water. There were dragonflies, great yellow and black things that flew around at tremendous speed and from time to time pounced on small flies and tore them to pieces; also smaller dragon-flies, with blue and green wings, that flew about more slowly and feebly, and seemed to spend a great deal of their time just sitting on a piece of grass or rush. The workmen called the big dragon-flies 'horse stingers' and declared that they would attack horses; but neither I nor any of them ever saw one do so. In April the caddis-flies hatched out and, as one walked through the rushes, they would flutter out in scores. At the end of May, or, more frequently, the middle of June, the may-flies appeared. This was really a most remarkable event. They varied in numbers according to some peculiarity of the weather; or perhaps floods or other causes during the previous year or years. In some summers they would appear in thousands. Then was the time to stand on the bridge and watch the drama. Swallows and martins pursued them in the air and as they fell on to the water, dace, chub and roach seized and swallowed them.

The birds of the river, also, were usually more plentiful and varied than the birds of the fields and woods. In fact one might see almost any woodland or field bird near the river at some time or another, in addition to such birds as could be found there and nowhere else. The largest of all the water birds was the swan, of which species there was nearly always a pair on the shallows behind the mill. Almost every year the swans nested on one of the islands close by, raising a great heap of rushes as much as would fill a couple of wheelbarrows. The male swan was very jealous of a near approach to the nest and would snort and ruffle his feathers in a very threatening manner. Should a still nearer approach be attempted, he would hiss loudly and charge towards the intruder at such a pace that the water fairly foamed around him. Later on the cygnets would appear; charming little grey things. I believe that in most cases one egg out of a swan clutch was addled; at any rate, very rarely a year passed that I did not find two or three such eggs floating in the river. I was bringing one home in the boat one day and, stepping back carelessly, put my foot on it. It exploded with a tremendous noise and the stench was so great that I really do not know how I got the boat to the bank. Though I washed the heel of my boot in the river, then dug it into the soil, and then washed it again several times, I could not get rid of the smell, The boat was put out of action for several clays; the stench that hung about it was so terrible that nobody had courage enough to go near it.

Two common but interesting birds were the moorhens and coots. The coots spent a good deal of their time in small flocks except during the nesting season. The coots, when disturbed, swam or flew to some other part of the river. The moorhens, though often congregating in some numbers on a favourite feeding ground, lived in a more solitary manner and when disturbed each bird would fly to some known shelter beneath the bank, or in a rush bed. A moorhen surprised on the water usually dived at once and swam to some weeds, where it would remain with only the tip of its beak above water. When a coot had a nest somewhere near, it, too, would sometimes dive and swim beneath the surface to a place of safety. The coots made their nests in clumps of reeds or rushbeds standing in the water; so that the nests were always quite surrounded by water. They often used green materials in the construction and frequently pulled some of the rushes over as if attempting some sort of protection against attack or observation from above. The moorhens always used dead materials with which to construct their nests and built them in a variety of situations. Sometimes the nests were out in the rush beds, sometimes in the flags by the river's bank, sometimes on the low boughs of a tree overhanging the water. Quite a number built on the tops of the pollard willows. The farm workmen always referred to the coots as 'bald-headed coots,' the conspicuous white shield at the top of the bill giving them somewhat the appearance of being bald. Moorhens were usually called 'dib chicks,' which was rather confusing, as the little grebes were known to more educated people as 'dabchicks,' though local people referred to them as 'di-dappers', pronounced 'die' and being no doubt a contraction of 'dive'.

THE RIVER

There were always several pairs of dabchicks about the river and each pair seemed to claim one particular stretch to the exclusion of the others. When alarmed the dabchicks dived immediately. They rarely flew and, when they did, they trailed their feet along the surface the whole way collapsing suddenly at the end of a short flight and at once diving under water. Their nests were placed in the rushbeds out in the shallows, or at the edge of some pool, and appeared to be merely small heaps of rotting weed raised barely an inch above the surface of the water. The removal of the top layer of weed disclosed the stained white eggs. I never saw the eggs naturally uncovered; nor did I ever see a dabchick in the act of covering them. I therefore concluded that this was done with extreme rapidity directly anything suggesting danger appeared. These birds were always very shy and it was only during floods that one had an opportunity of watching them feeding at close quarters. At such times the only still water was in the mill tail and from the mill window one could then watch them diving and returning to the surface with small fish in their beaks.

A bird very similar to a moorhen in shape and colour but with a much longer beak and less than half the size, was the water rail. Water rails were said to be rare; but this was probably due to their extreme shyness. They were much more frequently heard than seen and, particularly in the nesting season, their really terrible 'railing' was often heard in the rushbeds and reeds beside the river bank. The country people called the water rails 'skitty hens.' Water rails were very rarely seen flying. Perhaps once or twice in a year one, surprised in a ditch, or disturbed by a dog, would take a short hurried flight to the nearest cover but more commonly they relied on their legs and it was often difficult to decide whether the small, dark object moving through the rushes was a rat or a bird. They were cunning creatures and, when hunted by a dog, would climb up into some bush, and from the safety of their perch, watch the dog trying to puzzle out the line of scent that had abruptly terminated where the bird left the ground for the branches of the bush.

Wild ducks nested every year on the islands and I can well remember the first nest Father showed me. It was in a bed of nettles on the big island and I marvelled at the softness of the down with which it was lined and which I was told the duck had pulled from her own breast. The wild ducks nested early and, whilst many other birds still had eggs, one might disturb the mother duck and her downy ducklings. Then there would be a great commotion, the ducklings scattering in all directions and the mother flapping away with dragging wings in an attempt to draw attention to herself

Pike leaping

and away from her children. The wild ducks nested in all sorts of odd situations. Their nests were never placed on the water; sometimes they chose a place miles away from any river or pond. Sometimes one nested in the high bank adjoining the long meadow and placed its nest on the top of a pollard ash. The tops of pollard willows were also used for this purpose. Nearly every year at least one pair nested in the bramble brake on the top of the downs at least two miles from the river. When the young ducks hatched out, the mother took them along road to the river. She always did this very early in the morning before human traffic appeared on the roads. It was really rather surprising that the ducklings could march this distance when only a few hours old. It was also surprising that they could drop out of the top of a willow tree, perhaps twelve feet from the ground, without being hurt.

In the winter, particularly during very severe weather, many more ducks appeared. Next to the wild duck, or mallard, the commonest were teal. These pretty little ducks chiefly frequented the ditches in the meadows. When disturbed they would spring into the air at tremendous speed, dash off across the meadows, whirl around in a close flock several times, sometimes high in the air, then sweeping down close to the ground; then quite suddenly they would dive down into another ditch. The speed of flight was well illustrated when one day Father allowed me to go with him when he went to stalk a flock he had seen on the river from a gap in the hedge on the road above the high bank in Long Ground. There was ice along the side of the river and it was difficult to move across the frosted grass without making a sound. We crouched low as we approached the river bank and suddenly seven birds shot up into the air in a line. Father fired and the last bird fell. I saw it swim under water to the shelf of ice fringing the side and had to be restrained from breaking the ice with my heel lest I should fall in. At length it was captured and killed. It was handed to me to carry home and all the way across the meadows I stroked the sleek, tight plumage and admired the delicate pencilling of the flanks, the green patch on the wing and the green, yellow and velvety red of the head. As soon as we reached home I began to explain to Mother what a wonderful shot Dad had made. 'Not a very wonderful shot, I think,' he said. 'I aimed at the first and got the last!' There was also an occasional pochard and widgeon, and also a black and white 'diving duck' which I think must have been a tufted duck. Another occasional winter visitor which I have never been able to identify was a duck that appeared to be black and was referred to as a 'cur.' Pochards were 'duncurrs': so I suppose the black bird was closely related to them.

All the year the herons could be seen beside the river, beside the ditches and in the meadows. Eels were their favourite food; though they would capture and devour any small fish, animal or bird that came within reach. Occasionally they struck at and killed a pike too big to be swallowed. I once found one dead, with a pike of quite two pounds stuck in its gullet. They were very patient at their fishing and often stood almost motionless for an hour or two at one spot waiting for an eel or some other fish to come within striking distance. No other birds associated with them and they were frequently mobbed by rooks or peewits when flying over the meadows.

Occasionally a bittern was seen in the reed beds. It was at once pursued and, if it did not remove itself from the district, was certain to be shot. A stuffed bittern was looked upon as a valuable addition to the front hall. We could not have found a place for such a thing in our hall, which was merely a small space between the front door, the stairs and the two front rooms on either side.

Of the smaller waterside birds the most interesting, because of their beautiful little nests, were the reed warblers. The birds themselves were plainly coloured in warm brown tints with lighter underparts; but their movements were quick and graceful. Their nests were suspended between the stalks of the long 'spears' or sedges, and so constructed that, however severe the wind, they never spilled their contents. Sometimes, after the brood had hatched, Father would cut the stems of the sedges and bring the nest and its supports home. Then it would be stuck up in a corner one of the rooms.

The reedbeds were also inhabited by numerous sedgewarblers and reedbuntings. The jarring, jangling notes of the former could be heard all through the summer nights and, if for a while they were silent, a stone thrown into a reedbed in the dark at once aroused them to noisy protest. The reed buntings were known as 'spearsparrows' because, with their black heads, they very much resembled the common housesparrows. Though both these birds and the reedwarblers were summer visitors only, I once found a sedgewarbler's nest containing two fresh eggs on a Boxing Day.

Every spring sandpipers, which were known as 'summer snipe,' passed up the river. They were very tame and, when disturbed, would fly off with curiously arched wings and pitch again at the first convenient spot. Upon alighting they always at once ducked or bowed, once or twice, and then kept their tails moving in a manner very similar to that of the wagtails. True snipe were rarely seen except in winter and then not in any numbers except in very severe weather. Though there were plenty of boggy places in the meadows and beside the river, snipe seemed to frequent certain spots only. At times some of these particular places would be full of snipe and they would rise rasping and twisting in bunches of half a dozen or more at a time as one drew near. Although hard weather, or the approach of hard weather, usually brought a great many snipe to the district, their presence or otherwise did not appear to depend entirely on the severity or mildness of the time; but, when a great many were about during a mild spell, country people would say, 'They're having hard weather up north.' Here and there a little jack snipe would be found, always only one in one spot and very rarely anywhere near any of the larger common snipe. The meadow ditches were always favourite haunts of snipe in winter and every bare patch of mud bore evidence of their probing.

Wagtails of three sorts were to be seen. The black and white pied wagtails remained throughout the year and rarely strayed far from the farm buildings; their favourite spot by the water being beside the shallows at the back of the mill where the horse went to drink. In the summer the beautiful yellow wagtails came to the meadows, their bright colour in keeping with the glowing kingcups and buttercups. The grey wagtail, which has a grey back and a yellow breast, was only an occasional visitor, usually in autumn, and rarely stayed long. These occasional grey wagtails were evidently stragglers on migration. The pied wagtail nested every year in the faggot rick at the back of the bakehouse. Another favourite spot was in the thick growth of shoots that sprang from the upturned roots of an elm that had fallen to winter's storms. The yellow wagtails were said to nest beneath overhanging turfs by the side of the river; we often searched in such places, but never found a nest.

THE RIVER

A few sandmartins nested at one spot where the bank of the river presented a bare, upright face. In this they dug holes in which to place their nests. A great number could always be seen hawking over the shallows on their first arrival in April; but a few miles away there were large sandpits and railway cuttings through sandy soil which were much easier to dig in than the rather solid, clay-like soil beside the river and to which places most of the birds departed when their nesting time arrived.

The most beautiful of all the water birds was the kingfisher. Never plentiful, but always present, its rapid flight, brilliant colouring and piercing note always attracted attention. Every year a pair nested in a clay bank overhanging the river about half a mile above the mill. In summer the kingfishers chiefly frequented the little bays overhung by trees, from the low branches of which they launched themselves upon the passing shoals of minnows and small fish. In the shelter of such trees I frequently fished for perch and on several occasions, as I sat quietly waiting for a bite, a kingfisher came and perched upon my rod. In winter, and particularly when the river was full and coloured, the kingfishers haunted the ditches, up which many small fish travelled in order to be out of the turbulence of the main stream. After big floods many small fish were left in the depressions always found beneath the meadow gateways. The kingfishers soon found them and from the rails of the gates dived upon them as they swam round and round in their prison.

I did not have to travel far on the river to find all that I needed of interest. Below the bridge there was a long, deep stretch of about half a mile which sometimes provided some good perch in summer and was a favourite stretch for pike in winter; but it afforded very poor feeding ground for birds and was rather too much of one type to be of great interest. Upstream and close to the mill the river twisted and turned in a series of pools, shallows and swift little runs that were infinitely varied in appearance and character and formed suitable haunts for almost every type of bird, beast or fish that used the river as its home or hunting ground. In this interesting and productive area I spent most of my time and was never at any moment more than a quarter of a mile away from home: so that, should I have forgotten some essential part of my equipment, or the time arrive to return for a meal, I had only to push the punt to the side, tie it to the nearest bush, and be indoors within ten minutes. Starting from immediately above the bridge, close to which the punt was always moored, there was first the shallows where the horses drank and where I could always find minnows, gudgeon or dace. Then, passing up behind the Little

Island, one came to First Hole; a fairly deep pool with a beautifully clear bottom and containing many good perch and a wonderful shoal of large roach. At the head of this pool was a large piece of the river's bank which had been cut away in a flood and settled in this spot. This lump of clayey earth was about four feet high, by about the same width, and perhaps eight feet long. It lay about four feet beneath the surface and under its shelter one could often find good perch and large eels. The river just above this spot took two sharp turns and, by reason of the swiftness of the current at the corners, was the most difficult part to negotiate with the punt. The only way to get this rather clumsy craft to pass these obstacles was to keep close to the reeds till the corner was reached and then shoot across to the opposite side and the stiller water there by one vigorous thrust of the pole. If the push was not well-timed or too weak the head of the boat swung round in the current and one was carried back to the tail of First Hole and had to start all over again. I generally allowed eager boy friends, who had no experience of punts but longed to prove their skill, the opportunity of proving that to manage a clumsy rush punt was not at all easy. After they had exhausted their strength by repeated failures, I would take the pole and quickly have the punt gliding over the still water of the deep Corner Pool.

Corner Pool was another wonderful place for roach and often held good pike. It was so deep that one could only touch bottom with the long pole in one or two places and the easiest way to propel the punt was by 'paddling;' that is, by standing at the head of the boat and sweeping through the water with strokes of the pole alternately on the right or left-hand side. I very rarely fished from the boat in this pool, because the roach lived close to the bank just below a ledge at the head of the pool and it was much easier to fish for them from the land. If one used the boat here one would have had to anchor it to the bank right over the place most favoured by the roach, and this would have scared them.

Next above Corner Pool came Stumps Pool and Pole Hole. Which were really two parts of the same pool. These two pools were at the tail of The Island. The first was distinguished by a row of stakes which originally helped to support the bank of the island, but which during my time had become separated from the land and formed a favourite spot for perch. Pole Hole must at one time have been part of The Island itself, or, at any rate, a part of it must have been connected with the land; for in its centre stood a single tall pole. This pole made a fine anchorage for the boat and all around it was excellent water for perch.

THE RIVER

The river here was divided by The Island. If one travelled upstream to the right, one first passed over Long Ground shallows and then came to a stretch of deepish, weedy water that extended the whole length of The Island and rarely contained many fish. But this stretch was worth traversing because at the head of The Island one came to Barn Pool which was also an excellent spot for either perch or roach. The Island was so called because, although there were plenty of small islands about the river, this island was of considerable extent and was probably fully a quarter of a mile long. Barn Pool was so called because it was exactly opposite the barn.

The water upstream to the left of The Island was of considerable interest. Passing through a narrow opening in a rushbed, one came upon a quiet, still and rather shallow pool that seemed quite shut away from the rest of the world. It afforded fairly good fishing; but claimed attention chiefly on account of its seclusion and beauty. It was known as Lower Island Pool. The river seemed to end there; but a twisting channel could be found at the head of the pool which admitted one to Little Island Pool, a place of very little interest to an angler; but held in some awe by me by reason of its being the scene of a very brave rescue by my Father when he was a boy. He was bathing there with some young friends, only one of whom could swim and that one only very feebly. The swimmer got out of his depth, lost his head and sank. Father waded in, struggled under water till he could reach his friend, then struggled back to the bank again. I have always thought that that was one of the bravest deeds I have ever heard of.

Next above Little Island Pool, came a great deep and sombre pool known as Rolling Bay Hole. The rolling bay itself no longer existed; but it had at one time formed the barrier which drove the stream down under the mill and kept up the head of water when necessary to drive the mill wheel. When the bay was standing the pool must have been an attractive, lively stretch of water, foaming at the head and the movement extending in sparkling ripples right down to the tail. But with the bay demolished it became a dead thing. Its surface was still and its bottom consisted of deep mud from which every few minutes blobs of green slime would rise. Though it contained perch and pike, I never cared to fish in it; in fact, I was afraid of it and, when many years afterwards I found that some friends were using it regularly as a bathing place, nothing would persuade me to join them there for a swim.

Yellowhammer

Chapter IV
Hedgerow Birds

HE gayest and commonest of all the hedgerow birds were the chaffinches. They were certainly more common than the sparrows; but, because they flocked only in the winter months, and even then not all of them, they did not appear to be so numerous until one went about purposely looking for them and comparing with the number of sparrows seen. Their nests were marvels of neatness and one could be found in almost every hundred yards of hedge. Many also nested in the lower branches of trees, apple trees being great favourites. The outsides of the nests were entirely covered with pieces of grey lichen and, when placed in a fork of the branches of a lichen-covered apple tree, were most difficult to find. The cocks were magnificent little birds, having almost every colour in their feathering. In full plumage I have always considered a cock chaffinch one of the most beautiful birds in the world. Their cheerful song, always ending with 'Kiss me dear,' was one of the first signs of coming spring. According to most authorities the sexes separate during winter. Though this may be a general rule, and one could almost always rely on seeing a flock consisting entirely of cock birds in the beech avenue towards the downs any time during the winter months, around the farm both sexes remained together throughout the year and, during hard weather, several cocks and hens could always be seen in the mixed flocks of sparrows and greenfinches that frequented the rickyard and farm buildings.

Greenfinches also were very common. They were handsome birds; chiefly dark green with a splash of bright yellow across the wings. Their nests were not nearly so attractive as those of the chaffinches, nor was their song so cheerful; it being a rather plaintive sort of wheezing sound. In summer, they could be seen in ones and twos anywhere along the roadside hedges and in winter they collected in flocks and frequented the rickyards, where they hunted for food amongst the chaff and litter left after threshing.

Another bird mostly seen about the roadside hedges was the yellowhammer, always very conspicuous in its bright yellow garb. The yellowhammers made their nests in the banks and always advertised their situation by sitting on the highest bramble spray close by and continually repeating their rather plaintive song about 'a little bit of bread and no cheese.' The country folk called them 'scribbling larks' because their eggs were marked with little dark blotches, trailing off into thin, straggling lines; as if someone with an unsteady hand had tried to make dots with a pen and had been unable to prevent the pen from scribbling a tail to the dots. They had distinct territorial boundaries. Each pair kept to its own particular stretch of road and, although there seemed to be no squabbling about it, neighbouring pairs rarely went outside their own selected domain. There were, perhaps, six or eight pairs of yellowhammers living within a quarter of a mile of the farm. Further afield the yellowhammer population became thinner, until the neighbourhood of another farm was reached. They did not seem to care to live far from human habitations.

Robins nested amongst the moss and violets on the banks beside the roads. There were certain spots particularly favoured; every year a robin's nest would be found within a few yards of the same spot. We got to know of these places and always began our search for the nests as soon as the first violets appeared; for the robins were early nesters. But we never touched their eggs. There was something almost sacred about a robin. Perhaps it was because we had been taught the rhyme:

> 'The robin and the wren
> Are God Almighty's cock and hen.'

We always spoke of robins as 'cock robins,' 'robin redbreasts,' or 'Bobbies.' The robins often became very tame and would come close to the back door seeking scraps of food. Sometimes one was pounced on by a cat; but I never knew a cat to eat one.

Wrens chiefly favoured ivy-covered trees as nesting sites and in such places built very cunning nests, domed, and with a small hole in the side just large enough to admit the bird. Many of these nests never held eggs, and were always known as 'cock's nests.' The wrens were busy, vigorous little birds. Their song was so tremendous for such a very small creature that it seemed as if the sound of it would burst them. They were never seen more than a few yards distance from a hedge, in and out of the shelter of which they would pop like little mice. They sometimes roosted in

HEDGEROW BIRDS

Hedgesparrow

the holes made by rats in the thatch of the buildings; but I think they were always careful to choose a hole that was no longer used by the maker. Seeing several follow each other into a hole under the low eaves of some cow stalls, I put my hand in. The cavity seemed full of little birds. I expect the poor little things were terrified as I passed my fingers over them; but not one of them flew out when I withdrew my hand.

Another bird that was never seen far from the hedges was the hedge-sparrow: a dark, grey-brown little bird with a curious habit of shaking its wings which had earned it the name of 'Shuffle-wing.' The beautiful blue of the hedge-sparrow's egg was always a source of wonder and admiration. There was a popular belief that the hedge-sparrow was the commonest victim of the cuckoo as a foster-parent to this bird's young; but my own observations later did not confirm this. Hedge-sparrows seemed to prefer to live at no great distance from the garden and buildings, and cuckoos usually preferred to keep to the more open country. Meadowpippits', robins' and sedgewarblers' nests seemed to be their more usual choice, pied wagtails, also, were often victims. Tits were everywhere, and of several kinds; great, blue, coal and long-tailed, Every hole in a tree seemed to have a tit's nest in it in early summer; but the long-tailed, or bottle-tits, made nests somewhat like those of the wrens and placed them in low bushes. The bottle-tits' nests were extremely neat structures, oval in shape, covered on the outside with grey lichen and lined with feathers. One feather usually showed at the mouth of the hole by which the parent bird entered. I could never understand what became of the long tail of the bird when it sat on its nest, I always supposed that it was kept turned back over the bird's head. In winter the tits congregated in small flocks. The long-tailed tits kept to themselves, and often twenty or so could be seen twisting and turning about in the roadside hedges and jerking after each other in bounding flight as the flock moved on. They maintained contact with each other by keeping up a thin, needle-like piping as they hunted for food. The other small tits often went about in mixed flocks. But the great tits were never seen in a flock, except, perhaps, as a family party of parents and young in early summer. The great tits were strong, aggressive birds and their smaller relatives always endeavoured to keep out of their way as much as possible.

Linnets were not common in the hedges. Their favourite haunts were in the bramble and gorse brakes on the downs. But a few always nested about the farm, generally in the low bushes that bordered some of the meadow ditches, and small flocks of them used the hedges as roads in their travels about the country during the winter.

A great favourite was the whitethroat, or nettlecreeper. The whitethroats were summer visitors only. They had a delightful habit of throwing themselves into the air from the top of a hedge and singing as they floated down again to their perch. They nearly always nested in nettle beds and quite close to the ground; a bunch of nettles growing in a dry ditch was a favourite site. They were extremely fond of raspberries and, to keep them and other birds from the fruit, a framework had been built so that the raspberry plot could be netted. The uprights for this 'cage' were stout willow poles and these, having been planted green, took root and each year sent out bunches of leafy shoots at their tops. There was an advantage in thus having live posts to the cage, as they did not rot and were firmer in the ground than any dead post would likely to be.

Other summer visitors were chiffchaffs and willow-warblers. Both birds were looked upon as sure harbingers of spring. The first sang its name repeatedly from the top of a tree; the second more frequently warbled its little downward scale from the wildrose thickets or ash poles. Occasionally a blackcap appeared and its most favourite situation was in the great bramble, rose and blackthorn thicket in the chalk pit. A beautiful singer was the blackcap; almost equal to the nightingale, the nearest haunt of which was two miles distant:

The wryneck arrived with the cuckoo and for that reason was called the cuckoo's mate. It usually sang its unmelodious song, 'pee-pee-pee,' from the top of a very high elm. It was an extremely shy bird and never allowed a very close approach. Even when on the top of a very high tree, it would drop from its perch and disappear as soon as it found itself observed. Its colouring also assisted considerably in hiding it, the feathers being beautifully mottled with greys and browns, so arranged that the motionless bird could not be distinguished from the bark of the tree amongst whose foliage it was skulking. Wrynecks were not common; never more than one pair on the farm and the next pair probably located nearly a mile away. I am told that they are now still scarcer in that neighbourhood.

Blackbirds, songthrushes and mistlethrushes were about the hedges all the year round. The last-named was the earliest singer; the first the latest. As early as February the mistlethrush, or 'storm-cock,' started his wild and rather mournful song from the top of the most exposed tree he could find. Swinging backwards and forwards in the gale he flung his monotonous phrases across the bare fields. He was no harbinger of warm days; frequently snow began to fall even as he sang. The blackbird, on the other hand, always seemed to know when settled spring weather was at hand. On a mild evening he would perch upon an ash pole and pipe a careful selection of his best notes. Between each phrase he would pause as if to consider what arrangement he should use for next effort. The songthrush, apparently well-satisfied with his composition, repeated each phrase again and again, before passing on to the next variation. Blackbirds were always known as 'blackies;' but songthrushes and mistlethrushes were usually referred to by their proper names.

It was Father who gave me a real interest in birds. He knew most of them, both by sight and song; and he was very good at finding their nests. He would often draw my attention to the song of some little warbler; or point out some seasonal visitor on its first appearance. In the spring he would show me any nests he found and hold me up to look into them: but he always said, 'I shouldn't touch them, if I were you: the mother bird will know and will then desert.' Later on, when I began to collect eggs, I would sometimes say, 'Oh, I would like to have one of those. I haven't one in my collection.' And Father would say, rather grudgingly, as I have since realised, 'Well, you can take one then, if you like; but mind you don't disturb the nest in any way, and don't break the branches or plants around it.' He tried to keep the locality of the nests hidden from those human and other enemies who might destroy the contents. It is only latterly that I have begun to understand how very fond of birds he was, and what an excellent observer he must have been. I know that he never possessed any book on birds; so that everything he knew about them, and that was a very great deal, was the result of his own observations and what he had picked up in conversation with others who had similar interests.

'Wild ducks'

Chapter V

Birds of the Fields and Buildings

REES in the meadow were limited in number. A few scattered thorns, some alders in places along the ditches, some willows (most of which were pollarded) and sometimes an elm or two in the higher parts; consequently most of the birds found there ground birds. Certainly the most regular meadow birds were the peewits. They nested there in the spring and flocked there in the winter. As soon as the kingcups in the damp spots beside the ditches began to show a hint of yellow in their swelling flower buds, the peewits began their courtship flights. Swooping and diving at tremendous speed they sent forth their rollicking cry 'pee-a-wit-twit-wit'. For hours at a time they tumbled, dived and twisted over the broad spaces of the meadows. Even after mates had been taken and some shallow depression selected as a nest, the love flights continued. The rich brown, rather large eggs, four in number and very pointed at one end, were so arranged, with pointed ends inwards, that they occupied very little space and so could be covered more easily by the relatively small bird. The darker brown, almost black markings were concentrated towards the broader end of the egg and there formed a well-marked ring. It was unfortunate that just at the peewits' egg-laying time the meadows had to be rolled. Though the man in charge of the roller usually kept a look-out for the eggs and sometimes appropriated them for his own use, they were so much like the ground on which they rested that they were difficult to detect and many were destroyed. In the winter the peewits, or green plover, were often joined by their relatives the golden plover. The latter were winter visitors only and were very different from the peewits in appearance, habits and notes. The peewits looked black and white when seen from a distance; though when observed close at hand one could see that their backs were dark green and that there was a distinct patch of orange near the tail. On their heads they carried a long pointed crest and their wings were distinctly rounded at the extremities. The golden plovers were brownish on the back and head, and spotted all over their upper parts with flecks of gold. Their wings were pointed, they had no crests, and their note was a shrill, wild whistle. The golden plovers were extremely swift in flight and when one of a flock turned, all the others turned at the exact same second; so that at one moment the flock looked white as the birds showed their undersides and the next moment it was difficult to distinguish them from the ground beneath by reason of their mottled upper plumage.

When the grasses in the meadows became ripe, pigeons came there to feed on the seeds and would rise up with a loud rattle of wings when disturbed. A good many pigeons nested in the scattered thorn trees, laying their two white eggs on a flimsy platform of sticks which, in spite of its apparent insecurity, always seemed to keep the eggs perfectly safe. Baby pigeons were the most ugly of all young birds. The pigeons were great drinkers and, even when they had no more young to rear and all the meadow hay had been cut and carried, they still came there to drink once or twice a day, usually selecting a large willow in which to pitch and from which to see if the coast was clear before descending to the water's edge.

The wide open spaces of the meadows made good hunting ground for various hawks. From on high they could clearly see any bird, insect or animal suitable as prey. Kestrels hovered and circled, ranging all over the meadows in search of mice and beetles. Sparrowhawks chiefly frequented the high thorn hedges, under the shelter of which they could often surprise a blackbird or thrush. Occasionally they struck down a peewit or moorhen Sometimes a peregrine falcon appeared. When one of these birds passed over the meadows, flying swiftly and high in the air, consternation spread amongst the other birds; the partridges crouched close to the ground, the thrushes and blackbirds dived into the thickest hedge and the peewits rose in a close flock and flew so high that they were almost out of sight. A pair of peregrines spent the whole of one winter in and around the High Wood on the downs and could often be seen hunting the woodpigeons as they came there to roost. The pigeons seemed to know that they would be safe amongst the trees and raced at tremendous speed to get there before the falcon could make its stoop. Sometimes the pair worked together and, singling out a pigeon, one falcon would drive it so that the other could cut it off in its flight. The second falcon would descend at terrific speed and a cloud of blue feathers floated off on the breeze as the dead pigeon crashed to the ground. But, in spite of the speed of the peregrines, it was surprising how often the pigeons made good their escape. The peregrines always selected as their prey a fast-flying, bird; they seemed to despise any that were not skilful or rapid on the wing. The kingfisher, with its arrow-like fight, was always a temptation and at times a victim; though as a meal it could have been scarcely satisfying to such a comparatively large bird as the falcon.

Once a pair of ospreys took up a position on the top of a dead tree and from there flew up and down the river in search of fish. On sighting a fish near the surface, they would fall like stones and sending up a shower of spray, grasp some small pike or roach and lift it from the water. They remained in the neighbourhood for a few weeks only, but their coming was an event and I am glad to say that they moved on without being molested. Years afterwards I bought a book on Natural History and found therein a record of two ospreys seen in my home neighbourhood about the same time as these two must have been hunting our river. I like to think that these were probably the same birds.

Cuckoos haunted the meadows in early summer, hunting for the nests of sedgewarblers; they also found and used the nests of the meadow pip-its. The cuckoos much resembled sparrowhawks in size and shape; but their wing-beats were more rapid and their flight obviously more laboured. The hens, which could be distinguished by their chuckling, bub-bling note, never seemed to be as plentiful as the cocks. Often the cuckoos laid eggs in the nests of the skylarks, of which there were a great many nesting in the meadows. A skylark soaring upwards and singing was always watched by us with interest, in spite of the fact that it was an ordinary daily occurrence during summer and one could frequently see several high in the air at the same time. Of the cuckoo we used to say:

> 'In April come he will,
> In May he sings all day,
> In June he'll change his tune,
> In July away he'll fly,
> In August away he must.'

and also:

> 'The cuckoo is merry bird, he sings as he flies.
> He brings us good tidings and tells us no lies,
> He sucks little birds' eggs to keep his voice clear,
> And he'll come again in the spring of next year.'

I often hid under a willow in the meadows and called the cuckoos to the tree by imitating their note. It was then that I noticed that they jerked their tails up each time they called and that they never opened their beaks when calling. This discovery made wrong all the pictures of cuckoos I had ever seen; they were always drawn with their beaks wide open. But I never mentioned it to anyone as I was afraid of being jeered at for thinking that I knew more than other people about such things. Everyone seemed to have an extraordinary reverence for anything seen in a book; to be able to say, 'I read it in a book' was taken as proof positive that the thing must be true. But I made a resolve that, if ever I made a picture of a cuckoo calling, the bird should have its beak closed, no matter what anybody thought or said about it.

The high thorn hedges and isolated thorn bushes were very attractive to bullfinches and butcherbirds. It was easy to call the cock bullfinch by hiding under the hedge and imitating its single piping note. Then one could admire at close quarters the rose-pink breast and velvet-black head. The butcherbird's larder was a gruesome, but interesting, find. There one might see beetles and even small birds or animals spiked on thorns and awaiting such times as the bird ran short of food. The eggs of butcherbirds varied considerably in colour, ranging from a greenish to a pinkish shade.

During early summer nights a queer, rasping call, repeated for half an hour at a stretch, could often be heard in the meadows; one very rarely saw the originator of the sound, though once or twice the bird came peeping and creeping close to me as I lay still and hidden in the high grass. The corncrake trusted chiefly to running to take it from danger and, when it did decide to fly, it flopped away with its legs trailing, looking as if it could scarcely travel a hundred yards by that method. Yet it came across the seas to this country every spring and left by the same route every autumn.

In winter enormous flocks of starlings worked the meadows, the hinder members of the party rising and pitching again in front of the others; so that the whole flock seemed to be rolling across the grass. Fieldfares also came there in winter; but they adopted a very open formation and kept in touch with each other by frequent cries of 'chack, chack.' When flying from one part of the country to another the fieldfares moved in a widely-spaced flock, not in a close bunch as the starlings did, and kept calling to each other the whole time. These cries were often heard at night and Father would say next morning, 'We are going to have some hard weather; I heard the fieldfares passing over in the night.' Often the fieldfares fed on the red berries of the haws and a score or more might be seen hopping about amongst the shining fruit in some of the old thorn trees.

Thistles and teasers grew in waste places and to them came goldfinches, sometimes in flocks of fifty or more individuals. They were lovely little birds and showed the splashes of bright yellow on their wings as they danced away from one thistle-group to another. A certain amount of bird-trapping was carried on in odd moments by some of the men. The trap-cage and tame decoy was the method employed; but not a great many goldfinches were taken by these methods. I think that bullfinches were the commonest victims. The clap net, a much more destructive method, was formerly employed and to such an extent that goldfinches began to get quite scarce.

Though the treecreeper is usually looked upon as a woodland bird, a nest could nearly always be found somewhere about the meadows, and always in the trunk of a pollard willow. The old trees invariably cracked and split, and, in the earlier days of their decay, provided such suitable nesting sites for treecreepers that it was not surprising that at least one pair every year decided to make use of one of these snug crannies.

Every summer a pair of flycatchers would be found somewhere in the meadows. The high bank in Long Ground was a favourite spot; or the bramble thicket in the chalk pit. They seemed to be half asleep as they sat humped up on a conspicuous branch or post. Then an insect would pass and they would suddenly wake up, dive with a graceful curve at the insect and, having captured it, return to their post and resume their former sleepy-looking attitude.

The nearest woods were more than a mile away from the farm, so that woodland birds were rarely seen there. Very occasionally a green wood-pecker, or a nuthatch, came to the big trees in the garden during the winter; but neither stayed there more than an hour or so. The river attracted a few pheasants. Pheasants like rushy places near water and, once having found the river from some wood near its banks, they would follow its course by day and roost in the rushes at night till eventually they found themselves some miles from their original home. The big island was the usual location of any pheasant that came to the farm. As the island could only be reached by boat and was rarely visited, except at the time of the apple harvest, it was a quiet and safe spot for the greater part of the year.

Partridges were plentiful, particularly about the cultivated fields on the higher ground. Their nests were placed in the long grasses at the foot of the hedgebanks and were very difficult to find. A sitting partridge, disturbed by the too near approach of a human being, would flutter away as if with a broken wing, hoping by this means to draw the intruder away from her nest. After the corn had been cut and carried, the partridges frequented the stubble for fallen grain, retiring during the heat of the day to the cool shelter of a field of roots. When the stubbles had been ploughed, the partridges travelled further afield and could often be found in the pastures feeding on clover shoots, or in the meadows feeding on grass seeds.

Woodpigeons came in flocks at certain seasons of the year. A patch of wheat beaten down by a heavy thunder shower was sure to attract them. They would also come to the cornfields when the sheaves were standing in stocks waiting to be carried. As soon as the grasses began to ripen in the meadows, the pigeons went there; and in winter, when other food was scarce, they would come to the swedes and kales and fill themselves twice a day with the green tops. When there was a big crop of acorns, they went to the oak woods; beech mast also attracted great quantities of pigeons. A few turtle-doves joined the pigeons in the cornfields during summer; they were said to be quite harmless and to feed only on the seeds of weed; at any rate they were not sufficiently numerous to do serious damage and were such graceful little birds that no one cared to shoot them. A pair of turtle-doves bred nearly every year in the chalk pit, making their slight nest only about four feet from the ground in a clump of dogroses that grew on the sloping bank; a most suitable setting for such a lovely bird.

Rooks and gulls were always regarded as farmers' friends, because they followed the plough and devoured an enormous quantity of worms and grubs. But the rooks sometimes did considerable damage by tearing off the thatch of corn ricks to get at the grain. Occasionally a rook took to egg stealing; the gun was the only cure for that. Such a bird would watch a duck or hen and pounce upon its egg directly it had been laid, sometimes going inside a shed to do so. They also did damage to potatoes grown in the fields, digging up and carrying away the smaller tubers and pecking holes in those too heavy to be removed. Walnuts were a very favourite food and several rooks had to be shot every year to keep the others from robbing the tree that stood at the back of the mill. When they attacked seed corn, a boy was often employed to frighten them away. He was known as a bird-starver and was sometimes furnished with a large wooden rattle; or even an old muzzle-loading gun and some caps and black powder. Occasionally an adventurous lad would collect a handful of small stones and drop them down the barrel of his weapon on top of his charge of powder. I never heard of one of these lads killing a rook; but I have heard the stones rattling in the hedge and whistling over my head as I passed down the road just as the weapon was discharged. If the boy had neither rattle nor gun, he had to fall back on his own voice and it was extra-ordinary the volume of sound that came from some of these youngsters. I have known them to be so hoarse at the end of the day that they could scarcely speak.

Gulls inland were supposed to foretell the coming of rough weather. In spring a certain number of sheep and lambs died. The carcasses were left unburied and attracted a few of the larger gulls, which came day after day to pick the bones of the dead animals. A couple of ravens sometimes came on the scene; then the gulls had to keep at a respectful distance. At night foxes or stray dogs tore at the flesh. Very soon nothing remained but the bare skeleton.

Jackdaws were most plentiful during winter when the sheep were fold-ed on the roots. They were always about the sheepfold, sometimes perch-ing on the backs of the sheep. The extra food given to the sheep at this time seemed to be the chief attraction. Kestrels and sparrowhawks took almost daily toll of the mice and small birds that frequented the fields. The methods of the birds were quite distinct. The kestrels hovered on win-nowing wings scanning the ground beneath them; then, when they had located some beetle or vole, they dropped straight down upon it. The spar-rowhawks ranged far and wide, approaching under cover of the hedges and by their sudden appearance surprising some feeding bird. Sometimes they took quite large prey. One day one knocked down a partridge within six yards of me; I had disturbed the partridge from some clover and had no idea a hawk was anywhere near.

In my Father's young days quails seemed to have been fairly regular annual visitors to the district; but in my time they have become distinctly rare. The first I saw I mistook for a partridge chick and was astonished that a bird, apparently so young, should be able to fly so fast. I had two quail's eggs given me; but I do not know if they were found in my own district.

Golden plover, fieldfares and redwings were regular winter visitors to the fields. The golden plovers always came to the same field each year and always to the same part of that field. They had regular flight lines and any-one wishing to obtain a shot had only to stand at a certain spot under cover of the hedge at dusk. The birds in crossing to the next field were almost sure to pass within range of this spot. The fieldfares liked to feed on the ground left bare after the sheep had been folded on the swedes. The red-wings rarely fed on the arable fields; they nearly always came to the per-manent pastures and would certainly have been mistaken for common thrushes by most people. But the redwings were always in flocks of a dozen or more birds; sometimes fifty or more; whereas never more than two or three common thrushes would be seen together at one time. Watching them carefully one could see a flash of rusty red as they raised their wings in flight. Occasionally bramblings were seen with the winter flocks of chaffinches, readily distinguished by their white rumps. A much less frequent visitor was the snow bunting. I can remember seeing only three of these birds.

A rather heavy-looking, sparrow-like bird was often to be seen sitting upright on the top of a hedge. On finding itself observed, it would drop down to the other side and disappear. The cornbunting was fairly plentiful, but little noticed because of its dull colouring and shy habits. It was more frequently heard than seen, and this because it often chose to sing during the winter months. On any warm, bright day in winter a rather sad warbling song might be heard from some distance across the fields. It was usually impossible to get near enough to identify the singer and the discovery that it was a cornbunting was made only when one happened to be singing near some corn ricks, under cover of which I was able to creep near to the hedge. Skylarks were common all the year round and in winter their numbers were greatly increased by flocks which were said to be foreign birds.

The home-bred skylarks were believed not to do any harm; but the foreigners were said to be very destructive to autumn-sown wheat which was just beginning to sprout at the time of their appearance. On walking across a field of young wheat these foreign skylarks would rise in twittering flocks that must often have numbered many hundreds of birds.

Starlings were not usually seen much about the fields in spring and summer; but in winter the great flocks that were about might descend on any field. The starlings were always in a tremendous hurry rushing over the ground and stabbing hither and thither in the grass. They would stay perhaps half an hour in one field and then get up with a roar of wings and go skimming away to another field a quarter of a mile off, where the same proceedings were repeated. Sometimes they mixed with enormous winter flocks of peewits. Small parties would stay all day round the sheepfolds when the weather was at all severe. Because of their habit of staying about near the sheep, they were often called 'sheep stares.'

Except for a few robins, wrens, chaffinches, sparrows and pied wagtails which were always here, the birds frequenting the yards and buildings varied considerably according to the time of the year. In the summer swifts nested under the tiles of the mill, martins clamped their mud nests under the eaves and swallows placed their clay saucers upon the beams in the cowsheds. Martins also made their nests under the arches of the bridge. The sparrows were a great trial to the martins. Waiting till the nests were completed, the sparrows would rush in and take possession; the martins being no match for the sturdy and pugnacious sparrows. I was paid a penny a dozen for sparrows' eggs and twopence a dozen for the young birds and I found the arches of the bridge a very profitable hunting ground; but I always regretted that the sparrows had turned out the useful and pretty martins. There was really no excuse for this robbery either, as there were plenty of holes in the thatched roofs of the buildings in which the sparrows could have nested.

A barn owl often stayed about the barn and no doubt did good work amongst the rats and mice. It is probable that it would have nested there had there been a suitable place. A box or barrel fastened to one of the crossbeams of the roof, or fixed in a comer inside under the thatch, would almost certainly have found a tenant. A one-legged barn owl stayed about there all one winter. It had struck at a rat on the bank near the buildings and unfortunately put its foot into a trap set for the rat. The trapper had to throw his coat over the owl before he could get at the trap to release it. This owl spent most of the daytime sitting on the top rail of a gate and, rather strangely, I never once saw it mobbed by the small birds, as usually happens when an owl shows itself, in the daytime.

In winter the stackyards were thronged by swarms of sparrows, chaffinches and greenfinches. The harder the weather, the more birds came there for food and shelter On one side or other of the ricks there was always protection from the wind and, by diligent searching amongst the broken straws and chaff, a few grains of corn or weedseed could be found. When snow fell, close under the lee side of the ricks was often the only place where bare ground could be found. In one particularly severe winter small birds died in dozens round the ricks; many also fell victims to rats as they crouched close to the bottoms of the ricks. Most of these unfortunate birds were too frozen or starved to attempt to fly away and the rats just came out and helped themselves.

Sparrows nested in a great many different situations: under the tiles and thatch, anywhere where a fallen brick exposed a hole, in cracks and crannies in the old willows and in holes in the face of the chalk pit. They even built their nests, which were little more than great bundles of straw, in the high trees around the garden. Wrens could always be seen about the place, hunting for insects in the thatch and frequently coming inside the sheds to search for spiders. From time to time a moorhen overcame its natural shyness and fed with the fowls and ducks outside the mill; but it would never do so if any human being was close at hand. This I thought rather odd, because I saw moorhens feeding quietly close to people in a public park in a neighbouring town and the moorhens about the mill were rarely molested. Once a wild duck came to feed regularly for a week or more with the tame ducks. It soon recognised the call 'Coo-dill, Coo-dill' with which old Sam used to attract the tame ducks to their meal. The wild duck always walked up from the river to the roadway outside the mill where the tame birds were fed. One might have expected such a strong-flying bird to use its wings to come to the feast. Its action seemed to suggest that it was following the example of its tame relatives; as if it considered that they knew that walking was the correct method of approach. Even in their greatest haste the tame ducks rarely rose from the ground, though they might flap their wings vigorously to increase the speed of their running.

A tremendous elm tree grew on a plot of land between the mill and the river. Just before sunset during the winter months the top of this tree would become black with starlings. At first a party of about fifty would arrive and, as soon as they had taken up their positions, they would commence a great chattering and warbling. Every few minutes fresh parties would arrive to swell the company already on the tree and to add to the noise of their chattering. This continued till every branch on the tree-top seemed full of birds and the noise was astonishing. Then, as in response to some agreed signal, the whole company would suddenly burst from the tree with a mighty roar of wings and disappear in the direction of a copse some distance away that formed their nightly roosting place. The evolutions of the thousands of starlings that gathered at this copse were remarkable to watch. The whole throng moved as if conducted by one guiding mind, roaring down upon the nut bushes as if poured from a giant jug, then spreading out like a great fan and presently joining again to sweep in a living ribbon over the trees and fields. The performance took place nightly and continued for half an hour before the birds finally settled for the night. A few starlings nested in the thatch of the farm buildings; but never more than two or three pairs. They were not really common birds during the spring and summer; the enormous flocks of winter certainly did not consist entirely of birds of the district.

The pied wagtails seemed to find the neighbourhood of the buildings ideal ground on which to hunt for food; the domestic animals and their dung certainly attracted a great many insects. When not running swiftly about the road after flies, the wagtails usually spent most of their time on the roof of the house or mill. Sometimes they were seen on the thatched roofs of the cart shed or stables; but they seemed to prefer to be on the tiled roofs, perhaps because the tiles were easier to run, about on.

Robins came to the yard chiefly in winter; but never more than one at a time. Should a second appear, there was a battle at once and one or other had to retreat. The robin's usual perch was the top of the yard gate-post. From there it would cast its glance over the litter close at hand and, having detected the movement of an insect, would pounce down and seize it, returning at once to its perch to continue its watch for food. Sometimes one fell victim to a clever cat which used to sit in a fowl-scrape at the foot of the post and, though apparently asleep, seemed to know at once when a bird pitched on the post. It would then leap straight out of its little pit and often succeeded in capturing the bird. I believe it felt the slight vibration of the bird pitching on the post.

Considering the enormous number of insects and the amount of grain and other food always to be found about the yard and buildings, it was really rather surprising that the variety and number of bird visitors were not greater; but it was only the tamer sorts that had the courage to put up with the constant passing of human beings engaged in work about the place.

Very occasionally a flock of wild geese put in an appearance during the winter months. They were extremely wary and always kept to the middle of the broadest meadows. Father once saw a single wild goose feeding on a small plot of grass close to Pole Hole. He ran home for his gun, stalked and shot the goose. This was such an unusual thing to happen that he arranged a goose supper to which he invited a few friends. The bird was so tough that no ordinary carving knife would cut it and no one could eat it. Mother was particularly upset about this; but the guests took it as a great joke and the evening went off extremely well in spite of the failure of the chief item on the programme. This was the only wild goose that I have heard of as having been shot in that district and was probably a very old bird that had not strength enough to fly with the flock. A good many years later another solitary goose was seen in almost exactly the same place I once shot at some wild geese; but without success. I had been spinning for pike and intended waiting for flighting duck at dusk. As I was putting up my rod before changing to the gun my young brother who was with me suddenly exclaimed, 'Look at all the turkeys!' I turned round and saw a flock of about fifteen wild geese standing by some flood water about two hundred yards out in the meadow. I at once directed my brother to walk up along one line of railings whilst I walked along the next, so that the geese would be between us, the railings being about three hundred yards apart. I hoped that the geese would be confused by this and delay their flight until I got within range. They rose rather too soon but I tried a long shot. I did not get a goose, but the shot glanced off the water and hit my brother. They stung him, but did not break the skin. He was rather annoyed when I said, 'Well anyway, I did hit a goose.' I waited several nights trying to get a shot at another flock of about a dozen. On the fourth unsuccessful night I decided to change my stand from beside a withy bed to the shelter of a few thorns standing by the river. Just before it became dark I saw the flock pass over just clear of the top of the withies at the very spot where I had stood for three nights.

I knew of only one professional bird-trapper in the district and he followed it only as a side line to bee-keeping and sundry other jobs. Most country people were really fond of birds and it is pretty certain that any extensive trapping of song birds would have been resented. This man caught mostly bullfinches, to which no one objected as they were considered to be rather a nuisance on account of their habit of eating the buds of apple blossom. He used a tame call-bird and a trap cage. The cage consisted of two compartments. The inner compartment contained the tame bird and was securely fastened; the outer had a spring door which was left open, but which closed directly the wild bird stood on the perch inside. The cage was hung in a quiet thorn hedge when bullfinches were noticed in the vicinity and usually effected capture in a very short time. Quite a number of people had a singing bird in a cage at their door, some of the captives having been taken as nestlings and hand-reared. It was assumed that these hand-reared birds suffered no pangs at the restrictions of their cage, since they had never known a life of freedom. The chief favourites were bullfinches, goldfinches, linnets and thrushes. Jackdaws were sometimes kept and these birds often had complete liberty. Though very amusing, they were often extremely mischievous. I do not remember ever seeing a tame magpie; but that is easily accounted for by reason of the bird's extreme rareness in the district. My own trapping outfit consisted of a sieve, a stick and a piece of string. Sometimes in the winter I would rig up my sieve, scatter a handful of corn under it and retire to the shelter of a nearby building with one end of the string in my hand. When a sufficient number of birds had collected, I pulled the string and the sieve fell. I may have caught half a dozen sparrows as the result of a morning's work; but I certainly never made any very big bags. I soon discarded brick traps as I found that the commonest victims were robins and tits, neither of which birds I had any wish to destroy.

BIRDS OF THE FIELDS AND BUILDINGS

In a casual sort of way I noted the habits of the birds around the farm. I did not write notes, keep a Nature Diary, or follow any system; but every interesting habit once seen was always remembered and looked for again. The beautiful love flight of the woodpigeon was always a welcome sight and frequently seen from the windows of the house when a pair nested in one of the limes in the garden. The pigeon would fly at a sharp angle upwards out of the tree, then spread its wings and come swooping down in a long graceful curve, when it would again fly upwards and repeat the dive. The spreading of the tail of the turtledove as it rose from the ground was another action looked for: it was only when the tail was spread that its white edges and unusual shape could be seen. Sometimes I saw a kingfisher hovering above the water like a kestrel and then plunging down for its prey. The more usual way of making a capture was by sitting motionless on some branch, post or reed and dropping from there into the water. Moorhens were very pugnacious. Sometimes they were content with chasing each other about a meadow; but occasionally two would have a really serious battle, dashing about the water and making a great noise and commotion. In spite of this tremendous show of pugnacity, I never saw one of them any the worse for its fighting. Hedge-sparrows went about singly and were very quiet in their habits; but house-sparrows collected in flocks and seemed never happier than when making a great noise. It was not until many years later that I learnt that the hedge-sparrow was not a sparrow at all and that its proper name was hedge accentor; but I then preferred to call it by its country name of 'shuffle-wing;' 'accentor' seemed far too elaborate for such a nice, homely little bird. Rooks would let you walk by them without taking any notice, provided you did not carry a stick or anything resembling a gun; but if you stopped to look at them, they at once took fright and flew off. Treecreepers when hunting the posts in the garden started at the bottom of the post and worked upwards in a series of little clockwork jerks, then flew to the bottom of the next post and repeated the action. Peewits in the daytime and when not nesting flew steadily on their course; but when they flighted at dusk, they dived and swooped in a most erratic manner.

Hares

66

Chapter VI

Four-footed Beasts

OON after I had learnt to read I was given a book of Natural History. I found a great deal of interest in this book and at first felt I little discontented with the small creatures to be seen about the farm. I wanted to see big creatures like lions, tigers, elephants and, perhaps, a strange beast called a cameleopard, which I afterwards discovered was a giraffe. I had seen a bear, in fact, two bears. These creatures had come along the road one day in charge of a couple of Italians. They had danced to a concertina and sat up and begged. I was given a penny for each of the men and a small cottage loaf for the bears. I was really more afraid of the men than of the bears. I was timid of all strangers and these men were even more than that; for they were foreigners. The bears were muzzled and held by stout chains; so that I knew they could not hurt me. I could hear the horses snorting in the stables as they smelt the bears. Father told me that there was nothing a horse was so much afraid of as a bear. From my book I learnt that all breathing creatures were animals and that what I have always known as animals, as distinct from birds or fish, were more properly called mammals. The fact that most four-footed beasts reared their young on their own milk had been so constantly before me all my life that it excited no particular interest. I had seen cats with their kittens, dogs with their pups, cows with their calves, lambs and little pigs suckling, and even the women in the village sitting on their doorsteps with their babies at their breasts. These things were just as natural to me as the laying of eggs by birds. But the behaviour of all living things, apart from the natural functions common to all of any particular division of the animal kingdom, were the things that really excited my curiosity and this little book of Natural History made me eager to see creatures other than those inhabiting the country around me. In course of time this craving was partly satisfied by visits to the great annual sheep fair. This fair always attracted a great collection of the small showmen and in their little canvas booths I saw a great many strange creatures, monkeys, armadillos, snakes, various ferret-like animals, foreign wild cats and 'giant rats'; though even I saw through that deception. On one great occasion I was even allowed to hold a baby crocodile in my arms. But the most wonderful thing of all was the arrival of a real wild boar at the farm. Though it was really only a young wild sow, that made very little difference. Our landlord had brought it back with him from France and it was turned into one of our sheds until a suitable place could be arranged for it at the House. There was no doubt that this was a really savage animal. When I looked at it over the half-door, it would become almost demented with rage. Foam dropped from its jaws and it charged round its den snorting, grinding its teeth and tearing up with its snout the large pebbles of which the floor was made. It stayed there only a few days; Father was afraid of what might happen should it break loose and sent a message asking for its removal at the earliest possible moment. Other foreign animals that excited my interest were the 'buffaloes' that lived in an enclosure in the great walled park some two or three miles away and which I saw from the pony trap as I drove with Father to the great sheep fair. These were really humped Indian cattle and, though the bulls were said to be very savage, I don't think the cows differed much in behaviour from our own quiet beasts.

The number of species of animals, or rather mammals, to be found about the farm and fields was not very great and of these, rats and mice were certainly the most common. Mice, because of their small size, were not nearly so noticeable as rats; but threshing time often revealed that they were far more numerous than might otherwise have been supposed. When the bottom of a rick was reached, mice were sometimes found in scores. These were chiefly ordinary house mice; but there were often a few larger mice, with long tails and brownish-yellow backs, which were known as 'haremice.' These were long-tailed field mice and they were really quite as common as the house mice; but, by reason of their habit of remaining mostly in the hedges, were not so frequently seen. If rats were in the ricks, it was not usual to find many mice; apparently the bigger animals drove out the smaller. Another extremely common mouse was the short-tailed field mouse, which was really a vole. It was a dumpy little fellow with short ears and a short tail. It could be found anywhere in the hedges. One had only to lie down quietly by a sunny bank and presently the grass would be seen to move close at hand. A quick grab nearly always resulted in the capture of one of these little voles.

Rats varied greatly in their numbers. Sometimes the barns, ricks and banks would be swarming with them; then, quite suddenly, they would vanish. Occasionally great packs of rats, numbering hundreds of individuals, would be seen migrating to some fresh feeding ground. It was said to be extremely dangerous to interfere with one of these packs. Rats were always in the mill and these were always very difficult to catch. They seemed to be a resident population that had learnt all the dangers of traps. By a lucky chance I discovered how to outwit them. One day I saw an enormous eel pass up under one of the mill arches. I got down and crept along the mud that bordered the stagnant pool under the arch, hoping to find where the eel had gone. I noticed that the mud was thickly covered with the footprints of rats. I got a trap and sank it in the mud just under the water. Next day the trap contained a rat and, as often as I set a trap in that place, I was sure to catch a rat. As I was paid a penny for every rat's tail I produced, this discovery proved to be a very profitable one. Rats also infested the sides of the ditches and these I often killed by spearing. My weapon was made from an old rod-spear screwed into the end of a stout piece of bamboo. The rod-spear, which was a dagger-like implement which anglers sometimes screw into the butts of their rods so that they may stand them upright in the ground when not in use and so put them out of danger of being stepped on, had probably been left by some visiting angler. With this weapon I would probe the bank behind the rats' holes and so disturb the inmates, which would at once jump into the ditch and swim away under water. I soon became quite expert at spearing these swimming rats.

Commonly spoken of as the water rat, but very different from the true rats in habits and appearance, the water voles were plentiful along the banks of the river and in the meadow ditches. The land rat looked the fierce and sometimes dangerous beast it was: but the water vole, with its chubby face, small ears and quiet way, looked and was the opposite. At any time during the summer, water voles might be seen sitting on the floating weeds chewing the ends of rush stems. They were rarely seen more than a yard or two from the water and would dive and swim under the surface at the slightest hint of danger. The water voles' tails did not taper to a point as did the tails of the land rats, but ended abruptly in a blunt tip. Because of this they were sometimes called 'niptails' and an absurd story in connection with one of these creatures earned the title of 'niptails' for the inhabitants of a nearby village. The story went that a half-witted fellow of the village caught a water vole in a trap set for an ordinary rat. He had caught ordinary rats before and these he had killed by drowning; but it did not occur to him that it would be possible to drown a water vole. He

'Foxes were seen but rarely.'

enquired as to the best way to kill the creature and was told to tie a cork to its tail and fling it into the river, which he did, much to the amusement of the other local lads. But the story got into a neighbouring rival village and the inhabitants of the village from which it was supposed to have originated were not nearly so amused when they had to share in the ridicule by having 'niptail' shouted at them when they passed some of their rivals on the road or met them in the market town. Water voles were very rarely seen during the winter and I always supposed that for the most part they hibernated during cold weather.

Very occasionally another rat-like creature could be seen beside the river. It was almost black in colour and considerably smaller than the water vole; it also had a very pointed face. The existence of the water shrew was known to very few people. Even I saw but two or three of them and I think my good fortune in this direction was only because I spent so much time sitting quietly by the river fishing.

More often seen than the water shrew, by reason of its much greater size, the otter was known to everyone. But otters are extremely shy animals and, though the evidence of their presence could often be seen in their footprints in the mud, or the remains of fish on the river bank, relatively few people ever caught a glimpse of one. The most likely time to meet with an otter was when eel clatting at night. Then their whistle could sometimes be heard and perhaps one seen swimming down through the channels in the rushes. There was a hollow willow tree on The Island which was a regular haunt and I often went there just for the pleasure of seeing the animal slip silently into the water at my approach. Once I found an otter's slide in the snow and the tracks showed that the otters had had a grand time sliding down into the water and then climbing out again to repeat the process.

Foxes were seen but rarely. There were no woods near at hand and when foxes came about the farm it was chiefly during their hunting excursions at night. But occasionally one would be disturbed from a withy bed or clump of rushes in the meadows. Anyone seeing a fox immediately shouted 'tally-ho!' at the top of his voice, no matter whether it was in the hunting season or at any other time of the year. The hunting instinct was strong in everyone and the sight of hounds out for exercise brought everyone to windows and doors to watch them pass. The sound of the huntsman's horn was sufficient to stop all work on the place for half an hour or so; every man dropped his tools and raced to the nearest hedgebank, from which elevated position he hoped to see something of the passing hunt.

An animal considerably larger and also considerably rarer than the fox was the roe-deer. Roe-deer were fairly plentiful in the woods on the higher ground across the river; but the meadows were too open country to suit their tastes and consequently they very rarely crossed them. I know of one only that actually crossed the farm. This animal was seen to swim the river, cross the meadows, leap a gate into the road and another into the barn yard, then leap the rails out into the field beyond the yard and disappear in the direction of the downs.

The next largest animal was the hare, of which there were always plenty about the place. The fifty-acre field in which stood the barn was their favourite haunt. Here they could lie a good distance from the hedges and so see the approach of danger from afar. But, unless they had been much worried, the hares were not really very wild. They seemed to rely upon the wonderful way in which their colouring harmonised with their surroundings and one could often walk right up to a hare in its form before it would take alarm. Although I was used to seeing hares in their forms and could spot them as quickly as most people, I have on many occasions walked within a few yards of one without seeing it, only becoming aware of the fact when it got up behind me. It was the eye that always first caught my attention; but I have often pointed out a hare to a companion and he has been quite unable to see it, though it was crouched in a bare fallow less than fifteen yards away. Even when the hares jumped from their forms at one's approach, they did not at once put on their top speed; but lolloped away in an easy, confident manner, as if quite sure that they could outdistance any pursuer should any attempt be made to catch them. In the winter they liked to make their forms, or seats, in fallow land, or stubble that had not been ploughed. In the autumn a field of seeding clover was a very favourite spot and I have on occasion turned up a dozen from a ten-acre patch. The meadows also were favourite winter resorts in places where there were patches of coarse grass. A few sometimes sat in the rushes along the river bank and very often one would be found in a withy bed. In the early spring they seemed to be all over the place, running about the fields, and even in the roads, in parties of half a dozen or more, which consisted of one bewildered female followed by a number of ardent males. The males at this time of the year fought much amongst them-selves, but rarely with any serious consequences; though sometimes fur would fly from the violent kicks of the combatants. Young hares were born with their eyes open and fully clothed with hair. I think they were all laid in one place when first born, as occasionally two or three very small leverets would be found crowded together in a depression in the middle of a field; but almost at once the mother scattered her family and visited each youngster in turn for feeding purposes. In a litter of three, all were said to have a white spot in the middle of their foreheads. I do not know if this has been found to be an invariable rule; but all the members of the only litters of three that I ever saw together had white spots on their foreheads. Sometimes a hare, surprised in the meadow, would jump into the river and swim to the other side. Though a hare was a fine big animal and made an excellent meal, I cannot say that I ever really enjoyed shooting them and I never killed more than two at any one time on the farm. Though they did a good deal of damage to the crops, it seemed a pity to kill such a lovely creature unless actually required for food, and a wounded hare made such a distressing noise that I have been quite upset for some time afterwards when this has unfortunately happened. If a wounded hare was pursued at once, it often got right away; though it probably died soon afterwards. A better plan was to watch it and see where it lay down. If left for half an hour, it rarely got on its legs again; or, if it did, it had become so stiff that it was not difficult to capture. Rabbits and hares were said not to agree together but this could not have been quite true, as it was nothing unusu-al to shoot three or four hares and perhaps eight or ten rabbits from one gorse clump on the downs. But I do not think hares ever fed on rabbit-infested ground; the hares did not feed close to where they lay by day as the rabbits did, but often travelled great distances to reach favourite food.

FOUR-FOOTED BEASTS

The rabbits on the farm lived chiefly in the chalk pit and in the high, bramble-covered bank in Long Ground, the narrow meadow that ran the whole length of the fifty-acre arable field, though separated from it by the road. There were a few small buries in other parts of the farm and almost at any time after harvest or through the winter half a dozen or so could be got by hunting the hedges with a couple of keen dogs. Occasionally a few would be found on The Island and to get there they must have swum the river, as there was no place around it where the water was less than eight feet deep. One very large rabbit became quite famous. It defied all my attempts to shoot it throughout the whole of one summer. 'Chorl' once tried to fall on it when he came across it sitting in the rushes; but it escaped by leaping into the river and swimming to The Island. George, another of the farm hands, once found it in a heap of manure. The manure had been carted out into the field and left there in heaps until a suitable time should arrive when someone could be spared to spread it. George was put on to this job and in the course of his work came across a heap that had a hole right through it. He looked in at one end of the hole and, finding that he could not see through to the other side, knew that it was occupied. He debated whether he should try to stab the occupant with his fork, but decided that it might not go in deep enough, or might miss the exact spot. So, astride the heap, he inserted a hand into each opening and began to work them together. This loosened the dry dung and suddenly the rabbit burst through the top right into his face and raced away across the field. It was the same big rabbit that had defied my attempts throughout the summer to get within range of it with the gun. I eventually shot it one bright moonlight night as I was coming back from duck flighting on the shallows behind the church. It weighed four and a half pounds and I was really quite sorry I had killed it. Though I have since shot genuine wild rabbits weighing four pounds and a quarter each, I have never again either shot or seen one as big as this monster. The average rabbit weighs about two pounds and a half.

The rabbits in the chalk pit afforded me another curious experience. It was my half-holiday from business and I had intended doing a little roach fishing. The family had moved into Mother's house in the town[4] when I was about eight years old and Father had sub-let the farm house, retaining one room in which to keep his books and papers and do his writing. When I came into Father's office to get my rod, he told me that he had seen a rab-

---

4 In Rowlands Hill, Wimborne.

bit in the chalk pit as he came down the road and suggested that I should try and shoot it. I called the dog, picked up the gun and a couple of cartridges, and crossed the road. I soon saw the ears of a rabbit sticking up above the grass at the bottom of the clump of brambles that grew along the sloping side of the pit. I aimed below the ears and fired. I thought at first that I must have blown the rabbit to bits; legs seemed to be flying in all directions. The dog ran forward and began pouncing to right and left. I followed as quickly as I could and then saw the ground strewn with stricken rabbits, whilst I could hear another kicking and tumbling in the brambles. I saw that those outside were too hard hit to get away and tried to get the dog to go after the one in the bush; but it was too excited to pay any heed to my directions. I picked up six rabbits about three-parts grown and knew that a seventh had got into the bury to die. Father was astonished when I walked into the office a couple of minutes later and threw the six rabbits on the floor. 'But you haven't been gone five minutes and I only heard one shot fired!' he exclaimed. 'That's right,' I answered, 'and I only saw one rabbit; but there is another one dead in the bury by this time.' 'Well I've known people kill three with one shot before now and generally one or more of those has not been bigger than a rat: but six! and all fine rabbits! This the first time I have ever heard of that being done.' At harvest time it was a recognised custom to let the men have all the rabbits they caught. In those days selfbinders were unknown in our district and each sheaf had to be tied with a bond deftly twisted from a handful of straws pulled from the heap thrown out by the cutting machine. This entailed the employment of a great many hands and every available person was drawn in to work in the fields during the corn harvest, so that it took many rabbits to supply a couple to each person. As the island of standing corn got smaller and smaller, the men would stop tying up the sheaves and walk quietly along behind the machine watching for a movement in the corn, or endeavouring to spot a rabbit squatting there. Then suddenly one of them would fling himself flat upon the ground into the corn and more often than not he had a rabbit under him. Some of the men preferred to use a stick with which to knock down any rabbit they saw. When only a narrow strip of corn remained, the rabbits began to run out. But the changed appearance of the field bewildered them and very few had either the sense or the courage to run straight for the hedge. A crowd of shouting men and boys raced after them, sometimes pelting them with short sticks and stones. Many of the men could throw a short stick or stone with great accuracy and could knock over a running rabbit with ease, provided it was pretty close. Very few rabbits succeeded in reaching the shelter of the hedges.

In the winter rabbits were caught by means of ferrets and nets. Father would not allow a trap or wire to be set for them. He considered these methods cruel and proved that it was easy to keep the rabbits within proper bounds by other means. No one was allowed to go ferreting without a spade. The spade was used for digging out the ferret should it lay up on a dead rabbit, and for filling in every hole after the ferret had driven out the occupants. This appeared to take longer than the lazy, and usual way of leaving the holes open and going on to the next bury; but, as there were never any old holes left which might or might not hold a rabbit and so had to be tried in any case, one really covered the ground more quickly and caught more rabbits in proportion to the time spent. A good ferreter insisted on quietness during the operation. No stamping about was allowed, even if feet were frozen, and only necessary talking and in a very low voice. All holes were first covered with the nets, one end of the net being slung into the hole and the main part being spread carefully over the opening, care being taken to see that there were no thorns or brambles to catch it and so perhaps pull it clear of the rabbit. When all was ready the ferret was inserted and we could crouch down quietly close to the bank and out of sight from the holes. The rabbit bolting from the ferret struck the net with its head and that part of the net that had been slung into the hole flung up and caught about the rabbit's legs. As the rabbit rolled over tangled in the net, the watcher pounced upon it, and, seizing it across the loins, quickly broke its neck. Having disentangled the dead rabbit from the meshes, the net was carefully replaced over the hole in readiness should another bunny attempt to escape that way. When all the rabbits had been driven from the bury and the ferret had come out, every hole was carefully stopped before a move was made to the next place. On the next day's outing the original ground was traversed and any hole found opened was again stopped; as the rabbit that had dug itself out would then have moved to another bury or would be sitting out somewhere in the long grass or up in the hedge. I always tried to take advantage of this habit of the rabbits of sitting out in the grass after they have been ferreted, often with excellent results. Rabbits will also lie out when a stoat has been working their buries. When shooting over a ferret, the same plan of stopping the holes was followed and the shooter always stood in such a position that the rabbits bolted towards the stopped bury. No wounded rabbit could then ever escape by getting to ground; for finding the holes stopped, it became bewildered and was quickly caught and put out of its misery.

Many young rabbits were born in single holes dug in the middle of a field. These single holes were known as 'stops'; they were always quite straight and generally about six feet long. At the end of this hole a shallow depression was made and this was lined with fur pulled from the mother rabbit's body. In this warm nest the naked young were born and only visited by night, the mouth of the hole being usually closed up by the mother each time she left it.

Hedgehogs were plentiful; but rarely seen, unless discovered by a dog when curled up for the winter in a heap of dead leaves placed in a dry spot in a hedge. One dog we had always carried the hedgehog to some water and, placing it therein, caused it to unroll. The dog then seized it by its soft underparts and soon killed it. I did not allow my own dog to attack hedgehogs, as I had no particular grudge against them and did not like to kill anything just for the sake of killing. Hedgehogs did some damage by sucking eggs and were even believed by some to suck milk from sleeping cows; such cows were said to sicken and 'go off their milk,' meaning that the milk yield was much decreased after this treatment. Sometimes late on a summer's evening, perhaps when returning from fishing, I would meet a hedgehog hunting about in the grass. As soon as it realised that I was close to it, it would lower its head and sink into itself. Should I approach closer, the head would be drawn under and, should I touch it, the animal would at once roll itself up tightly into a ball. The gypsies ate hedgehogs and enjoyed them. The dead animal was rolled up in a ball of damp clay and placed in the embers of a fire. When cooked, the clay was cracked off with the spines and skin adhering to it. I tried this once and found the meat excellent.

Stoats and weasels varied considerably in numbers. The gamekeepers kept them down pretty well, trapping them in box tunnels set in the corners of the hedges; but they travelled a great deal and were often seen about the fields, or crossing the lanes. The stoats chiefly preyed on rabbits which they hunted down by persistently hunting one individual in and out of the holes and even across the fields, till the bewildered animal gave up in despair and sat down screaming to await the fatal pounce of its enemy. Sometimes the stoats entered the corn stacks for rats. On one occasion, when passing a wheat stack, I heard a squeaking up in the thatch. A rat emerged, ran down the thatch and leaped into the air. Close at its heels came a stoat which, leaping after the rat, caught it in mid air. The rat was dead when it reached the ground. Stoats also hunted the riverbank, slipping in and out amongst the rushes and darting out on feeding moorhens.

I killed one once which sprang out on to a moorhen I had just shot. I skinned and stuffed this stoat and have it still. I did the skinning early one morning before anyone was about; but I did not bargain for the stench from its scent glands and I was in considerable disgrace in consequence, the room being rendered quite unusable for several days. On another occasion I was bathing with some boy friends and saw a stoat leave the rushes by the river and go into the middle of a meadow, where it disappeared down a mole's run. The next morning, whilst we were bathing, the stoat came out of the same mole's run and made towards the river. I directed my companions to swim across and drive the stoat out of the rushes with their towels, whilst I stood guard over the hole. My intention was to catch the stoat alive; but, when I tried to prevent it entering the hole, it made such determined attacks on my naked feet that I was obliged to give way. Once when carrying wheat a stoat ran out from under a stock and was chased by my dog. The dog seized the stoat; but at once dropped it and vomited violently owing to the dreadful stench given off. This happened three times before the plucky dog succeeded in killing it. Father once saw a stoat carrying fowls' eggs into a faggot rick that stood beside the mill. He said that the stoat brought one egg at a time and seemed to be carrying it pressed between its chin and its chest.

Weasels were rarely seen far from a hedge and were so extremely quick in their movements that only a fleeting glimpse could be obtained of them amongst the herbage. More often they were seen crossing a road; their legs moving so fast that they always appeared to me to be moving on wheels. They could climb well and might sometimes be seen high up in the bushes. It was generally believed that, when doing this, they were hunting for birds' nests in order to devour the eggs or young. They were looked upon as farmers' friends, on account of the number of mice they destroyed.

Moles were plentiful in the meadows; but usually kept to those parts not affected by floods. Provided they kept to the permanent pastures, no one bothered much about them; but when they got into mowing grass, their mounds got in the way of the knives of the machine when the grass was being cut and so traps had to be set. A few of the old wood traps were in use when I was a boy. These consisted of a small box of wood open at both ends and with a slit in the top. A noose of wire attached to a strong, but pliant, stick was put through the slit and kept in place by a trigger; the stick being thrust into the ground near the run and bent down so as to form a spring. When the mole displaced the trigger, the stick straightened and pulled the wire noose tight about its body. I do not think the old wood traps were as merciful as the more modern metal traps; the latter grip the mole with tremendous pressure and must quickly crush the life out of it. Occasionally a mole with a cream-coloured coat would be caught. Dead moles were hung upon certain trees, after their tails had been removed to claim 'mole money.' These trees sometimes had several dozen bodies hanging from the lower branches.

More often seen dead than alive, shrews must have been extremely plentiful. No one seemed to be able to explain why shrews were so often found dead in the roads; but the popular idea was that they were extremely pugnacious and that, when two shrews of the same sex met, they always fought to the death. I was never quite satisfied with this explanation, as I could rarely find any marks of injury on the dead animals. I sometimes wondered if they died of rage. I knew small creatures could die of fright for I had often had a bird die without injury in my hands when I was trying to free it from the fruit nets in the garden. Certain old ash trees about the country were known as 'shrew ashes.' An earlier generation had believed that, if a shrew ran over a sleeping animal, the animal at once became afflicted, with a disease and could only be cured by being struck with a stick from a shrew ash. The curative properties of the tree were procured by boring a hole in the trunk and blocking up a live shrew in it. Cats would kill shrews, but would not eat them.

We recognised only three species of bats; the small bat, the long-eared bat and the great bat. The small bat frequently came into the bedrooms at night when the windows were left open during summer. Occasionally a long-eared bat would be found in the house, or in a dark corner of the mill. The great bat was much larger than either of the other two. It was only seen during the warmest months of the summer, when, just at dusk, it would appear flying high up in the air. Because of the height at which it flew it was often called the 'high-flier.' The bats squeaked shrilly as they flew around; but I found that this sound could not be heard by everyone, even though they might not have the slightest hint of deafness. Father explained that the pitch of the bats' squeak was so high as to be outside the range of many people's hearing. He thought that there might be a great many sounds like that which might be plainly audible to birds and animals, but not to humans.

I had a dreadful habit of falling down when I was a small boy. I expect it was because I was always thinking about something else as I walked along our rather rough roads. I was far too interested in the live things of the hedges to pay much attention to the ground on which I was walking; consequently, should I come to a projecting stone, I was pretty sure to trip and fall. Broken knees, slaps and a scolding were the usual results. Then I would limp along in a much more subdued fashion and wonder why it was that no wild animals ever seemed to meet with accidents. I can remember only one accident to a wild animal and Father said that he expected it had been shot at and wounded and had lost its usual ability through this injury. This animal was a roe-deer which was found dead in an old sunk lane at the dairy farm. It had slipped in going down one side of the lane and its head had been caught between two stout hazel sticks. I have since met with a few genuine accidents to wild animals, birds and insects; but, with the exception of the regular toll taken by telegraph wires, trains and motor cars, wild creatures have considerable ability in keeping themselves out of trouble in the way of accidents. Even when an animal has met with an injury it is quite remarkable how quickly it adapts itself to its handicap once it has recovered from the immediate effects. There were two hares that each lived for at least a full season in the neighbourhood of my home and managed to evade capture in spite of considerable handicap. One of these had lost a leg in a gin; yet with only three legs it managed to outdistance our dogs when they gave chase. The other had run into a wire snare and in its struggles had pulled out the peg. It was often seen running across the fields with the peg bumping along beside it; how it escaped strangulation I cannot imagine. Once my own dog nearly ran into it when the peg caught in a hedge as it bolted through a 'mesh'; but it managed to pull the peg clear just in time and again cantered away to safety.

Roach

Chapter VII

Fish

HE various species of fresh water fish were well represented in the river that ran past the mill. Altogether fourteen different kinds could claim to be regular inhabitants and, if we included the crayfish, a tench reported to have been captured in the hatch pool shortly before my birth and the occasional capture of a fish known as a bull-trout, which may have been a salmon kelt, a large brown trout, or a kelt seatrout, the number would reach seventeen.

Salmon, though passing up the river annually to spawn, were not sufficiently plentiful to be of any importance. In most years the parr, or young salmon, could be seen on the shallows, and every three or four years an adult fish would be taken by someone spinning for pike during the winter. Dead salmon were found fairly frequently after late winter floods. I once found one which must have weighed well over forty pounds when it first entered the river; it might even have weighed fifty or sixty pounds and was certainly by far the largest fish of any kind that I had seen up to that date. But they were too few in number and the river unsuitable in character to make salmon fishing a reasonable occupation. One was shot in a tributary stream under curious conditions. A farmer was walking along the bank with his gun and just as he reached a spot where two elms had been blown down across the stream, he saw a salmon leap the lowest tree. He held his gun in readiness and shot the fish as it attempted to leap the second tree.

Pike were the most valued of all fish in the river, both as food and by reason of the sport they afforded anglers. Many ran to a large size and every winter one, at least, of twenty pounds or over was captured. There were two recognised methods of pike fishing when I was a boy. One was by means of a live bait and gorge tackle, and the other by means of trolling with a dead bait gorge tackle consisted of two hooks lying back to back and attached to a length of twisted wire. The wire was threaded under the skin of the bait from the shoulder to the tail, so that the hooks lay along one side just behind the gills. A large float was used, and, when a pike took the bait, it was given plenty of time, perhaps ten minutes or more, in which to 'pouch' the bait before it was struck. The trolling tackle also consisted of a double hook, but had a long lump of lead attached to the wire. The wire was threaded through the mouth of a dead bait and out at the tail, so that the lead lay along inside the bait and the hooks stuck out on either side of its mouth. The bait was cast out into a pool and allowed to sink to the bottom; then it was raised a couple of feet, a yard or so of line recovered, and the process repeated. The pike in this case also was given time in which to pouch the bait before it was struck. Most of the pike taken by these methods had to be killed no matter what their size, as they were usually hooked well down in their interiors. It was rather extraordinary but, should one of these fish break away and eventually be captured, the hooks would be found inside and seemed to have caused it little inconvenience. Then came snap tackle and artificially spinning baits. With the snap tackle the strike was made most at once and with the spinning bait directly a bite was felt. Fish taken by these means were usually hooked in the mouth and could be returned uninjured if undersized. It became the custom to return all pike under about three pounds in weight. Father remembered the poke net in common use during floods. This was a deep net attached to a long forked pole. The net was lowered into the water in eddies, or close to bushes when the water was thick, and drawn towards the bank. The fish could be felt hitting the net as it darted out from its shelter; but not many really large pike were ever taken by this method, no doubt they lay too deep for the net to reach.

Doubtless large pike caused a good deal of havoc amongst young water birds and I have even known them dart at the dangling red feet of our Aylesbury ducks and send the birds flying and quacking from the water. The bridge was a fine place to study the habits of pike and other fish. When the water was clear one could lean on the parapet and look down to the bottom of the deepest pool. Young pike, up to about three or four pounds, were called jack; a diminutive also found in 'jack hare' or the smaller, male hare. One day a village boy was fishing from the bridge; he had his little brother with him. The smaller boy could not see over the parapet, so he took a running jump, intending to land across the top of the parapet so that he could lay there and look down into the water. But he jumped too hard and took a header into the pool below. His brother ran down to the mill for help and Father, shouting to the men who happened to be in the stable, to bring a cart rope, ran on to the bridge. The air in the small boy's clothes was keeping him afloat and

Father shouted to him to keep his hands under water and try to paddle himself towards the rushes; which he did. When the men came with the rope, the elder boy was lowered over the bridge and, drawing his young brother close to the buttress where he could stand, fastened the rope about him so that he could be hauled to safety. The rope was then again lowered and the elder boy attached it to himself and was drawn up. When Father asked the little boy his name, he said 'Jack.' 'Well,' said Father, 'I've seen a good many jack hauled up over this bridge; but never such a heavy one as this.' But the youngster was not to be pacified by any joking. His chief thought was not gratitude for his lucky escape, but fear of the whipping he would get from his mother when he reached home for getting his clothes wet.

Perch were fish for summer angling and a perch-fishing outing a regular treat once or twice a year. The chief baits were worms and live minnows; though I found later on that nothing could beat a small live gudgeon if big perch were about. Though perch could be found at times almost anywhere up and down the river, the favourite places were in Pole Hole and beneath some willows below the bridge. Pole Hole, which was so named because a tall post stood upright in the middle of it, was best fished from a boat which was tied to the pole and so gave access to almost the whole of the pool. When fishing for perch we had to be careful not to let a hooked fish escape, as this fish would then draw off the whole shoal. When a good shoal had been discovered it was often possible to capture a dozen or more before the remainder took fright. I discovered that many good perch could be taken from the openings between the weeds in the long, deep stretch below the bridge, by drifting slowly along in the boat and lowering my bait into every likely-looking space. Sometimes perch would be seen swimming close to the stonework of the bridge and feeding on the freshwater shrimps that lived there in the watermoss growing on the walls; but I never caught many when using the shrimps as bait. Normally the perch carried their spiny back fin lying close along their backs; but, when they sighted their prey, this fin was raised as the fish sailed in to make its pounce. A perch of a pound was considered a very good fish and one of two pounds, or over, was thought worth a glass case. One or two perch of three pounds were known to have been captured in earlier times and one of these stood in the hall of a large farm house about two miles further up the river. Pike were said to be afraid of perch because of their spiny backs; but later I found this to be untrue, as I sometimes caught pike with perch inside them.

Roach were the fish of next importance; originally because they were the usual bait for pike, but later because they gave one the chance of really delicate fishing. When I first started to fish, tackle was of a very heavy type and no one thought of attempting to catch perch without using a hook attached to a stout gimp. But occasional visitors showed us that good fish could be caught on much finer tackle, provided one played the fish carefully and used a net to land it. Then someone came along and, using a very small hook, fine gut, a thin quill float and boiled wheat as bait, began catching great roach of nearly two pounds. It was not long before I had found means (probably an accumulation of sparrow and rat money) of providing myself with the right sort of tackle and had started myself as a roach angler. I found it the most pleasant type of all summer fishing and have never lost my liking for it. The motion of the float indicating the shy bite of a large roach was very different from the sudden bob given when a perch took the bait. Often the float lowered only a fraction of an inch; but a keen eye could detect a slowing-up of its drift downstream. That was a sure indication of a large fish. At other times the float might begin to rise slightly as the roach took some of weight of the shot when lifting up the ball. To prepare bait, I put a handful of wheat into a cake tin filled with water and left it in the bakehouse oven for a couple of hours. The wheat would absorb the water and swell to four times its normal size. One, or at most two grains were placed on the hook and a few scattered at the head of the swim every fifteen minutes or so to keep the fish on the feed. Sometimes pike came into the swim. Then the roach ceased to feed for as long as the pike remained close by. Several times I have had pike rush out at a roach I was playing and carry it off. In the smaller roach the prevailing colour was a bluish green; the larger fish were browner and their sides a dull gold. With their bright red fins and polished metallic sides they were indeed handsome fish. In early summer their heads took on a grey-blue tint and became covered with little hard white pimples like chips of china. They often lay close to the surface at this time of the year and from time to time would chase each other through the weeds. It was their time of spawning.

Very similar to the roach in appearance when quite small, but differing considerably in shape, colour and habits as they grew older, the dace were also highly valued as bait for pike. They were rather more difficult to catch than roach, as they frequented much shallower water; but, as they often rose freely to flies, they offered the chance of a different type of fishing. Artificial flies were quite unknown to me as a boy, nor had I the right type of rod to cast them even if I had possessed them; but I devised a satisfactory means of catching dace with a fly by using the natural insect, a very fine cast and a long rod. Then, keeping out of sight and with the wind behind me, I would allow my bait to be blown out and alight in front of the fish. I often had good sport from the bridge when the may-flies hatched out. Then every dace was on the top of the water feeding eagerly on the floating insects and it was easy enough to get them to take the fly; but not nearly so easy to hook them. The dace had not the rich colouring of the roach, nor did they grow so big; a half pound dace was considered very exceptional.

Chub were very rarely seen close to the farm; but there were always some beneath the willows by the shallows behind the church about a mile further up the river. They grew to a large size; some being four or five pounds in weight. They were extremely shy and could only be caught by the exercise of great cunning and taking advantage of every bit of natural cover. They were at one time so uncommon that the first I caught was pronounced to be a cross between a roach and a dace. Returning to the neighbourhood many years later I was astonished to find the river simply swarming with chub. They were said to be clearing all the other fish out of the water, but, though roach were certainly scarcer, I think other fish kept up their numbers pretty well in spite of the great increase in chub. When we wanted specially to fish for chub, we used to go about two miles downstream below the next mill, where there were several good chub holes. We used a strange assortment of baits; cheese, grasshoppers, baked wasp grubs, paste, maggots, minnows, bluebottle flies, earwigs, and the disgusting beetle grubs found under cow manure. With artificial flies I think we could have had some wonderful sport.

Trout were so rare as to be of no consequence to the ordinary angler. The few that existed in that part of the river were mostly old and very crafty fish and could be seen for years about the same spots. I never heard of one being caught in my young days; but since then they have been taken occasionally higher up the river where they were more plentiful and these were, no doubt, escapes from a tributary stream into which they were introduced from time to time from hatcheries. An attempt was made to convert one part of the main river into trout water. In this part the stream was divided into many shallow channels and certainly looked ideal for the purpose; but I do not think much success came of it. Only a moderate number of the introduced fish stayed about the place; the remainder moved off into deeper water where the pike soon accounted for them.

From a food point of view eels were always highly esteemed. The next mill lower down the river had an eel-trap which let at an annual rental of one hundred pounds and often wielded over a ton of eels in a night. The trap was worked chiefly during the first autumn floods, when the mature eels were making their way to sea. We caught them in wicker pots baited with worms and sunk between the weed beds on the shallows. We also set night lines, angled for them in the ordinary way, trod them out of weeds into wide-mouthed baskets, and inserted baited hooks into their holes in the mud. But the most enjoyable and profitable way of catching eels was to go out during a flood or on warm summer's night and fish for them with a clat, or clot. The clat consisted of a quantity of worms threaded on to worsted and tied into a ball. This bait was lowered into the water in suitable spots and held just clear of the bottom. When the eel bit, a sharp tug was felt. The bait was then drawn up steadily but swiftly and in most cases the eel retained its hold till it was over the bank. It was a common thing to catch twenty or more eels by this method in the course of a couple of hours, if the weather conditions were suitable. Close, thundery weather was usually the best; a cold spell was quite the worst.

The only other fish that was angled for with any serious purpose was the gudgeon. Sometimes we went off on a gudgeon fishing outing. We used small floats, small hooks and carried a good supply of small red worms. We went in the boat and carefully examined the shallows and the edges of the pools until we sighted a shoal. Then we anchored a few yards above them and prepared the pitch by stirring up the sand and gravel with the end of the punt pole. The gudgeon worked up to the disturbed spot and started nosing about for food. Then we lowered our baits among them and very soon had a bite. But, though gudgeon are always supposed to be the most foolish of fish, we found that they quickly learnt the danger of a hook. After a time the survivors of some of our favourite shoals became so artful that it was quite impossible to catch them with a hook. It was then that I discovered that it was possible to snare them with a noose of gut. This was really quite a skilful method and required a steady hand and good eyesight. A dish of gudgeon, covered with egg and breadcrumbs, carefully fried and served with fried chopped parsley, was a real delicacy.

Minnows were extremely plentiful and, though not used as food for human beings, were most useful in the river as food and bait for other fish. I soon found that a 'bleached' minnow was a much surer bait for a perch than a dark one. In order to bleach the minnows they were placed in shallow water in the sun for about half an hour, when they would become quite pale in colour and show up very clearly in a dark hole under trees; the sort of place one would be sure to find perch on a hot, sunny day. One had to be careful not to leave the minnows in the sun too long, or they would die. Two minnows lightly hooked through the lips would tempt the shiest perch. The two minnows would kick about together as if struggling over a choice morsel of food and the perch invariably fell for this trick. Quite large pike could also be caught by the same method. In the early summer the minnows collected in vast shoals on the shallows for spawning. They then became very much darker on the backs and brilliant red on their throats.

Two other small fish might sometimes be found by turning over stones in the shallows. They were the bullhead and the loach. Both were probably quite common amongst the weeds, but were very rarely seen because they always stayed under cover. 'Bullies' were queer-looking little fish with very large mouths and heads. Loach wriggled quickly under the next stone when disturbed and were hard to hold in the hand because they were so slippery. They had fleshy whiskers on their lips.

Sticklebacks, or 'soldier minnies' were only to be found in still corners near the shallows; though they were common enough in the ditches. They built their nests in the weeds and the male fish then mounted guard outside. He seemed to be in a constant state of extreme agitation and could be seen hovering in the vicinity of the nest with his tail curved and fins rapidly quivering, ready to dart at anything that approached too near. At this time of the year, also, he was very brilliantly coloured; his head and shoulders glowing in green, blue and crimson. The colours became deeper when he became annoyed at the approach of a supposed enemy.

Every year I managed to catch enough lampreys to give myself a lamprey tea. No one else in the family would eat them; but I considered them a great delicacy. Towards the end of May the lampreys appeared on the shallows in little clusters of about half a dozen clinging to the stones with their sucker mouths. I never succeeded in catching them on a hook. My method was to wade in and creep up behind them; then grab them and fling them quickly on to the bank. I once came upon a bed of clay in the river that was full of them. Perhaps if I had searched carefully I should have found other beds of clay in which they resided and from which they could have been dug much more rapidly than I could catch them with my hands.

Crayfish may have been quite plentiful; but no one troubled to hunt for them. A few were taken in the wicker eel-pots; but never more than two or three at a time. These were always given to me and I generally managed to get someone to cook theirs for me. I expect I was considered rather odd in my likings for crayfish and lampreys: but I always had, and still have, a great liking for any sort of fish as food. Years after I had left my old home I read how people go fishing at night for crayfish with small round nets. I have often thought that I should like to go back to the old mill and see if I could make a good catch of these little freshwater lobsters by the use of these baited nets.

I did a great deal of fish-watching as well as fish-catching and found them most interesting creatures to study. I watched the cautious way in which a pike in open water will try to glide up to within pouncing distance of a shoal of smaller fish. Before the fish come near the pike is usually poised just clear of the bottom with its tail drooping in a listless sort of way. As soon as it notices the other fish its tail straightens out and its fins beat in a quick vibrating movement. It then very slowly turns until it is exactly facing its prey. Then it begins to move slowly forward. The pike has to get very close to be sure of making its capture. Sometimes the smaller fish seem to feel it coming; their movements begin to show slight agitation, they begin to close in and move forward. If the pike sees you standing on the bank and you make no movement, it seems to think that it has not been observed. It will then slowly back-water with its fins and so swim backwards until it is out of sight or has come close enough to a weed-bed to make it safe to turn quickly and dive under cover. An eel will also sometimes swim backwards when alarmed; but it differs from the pike in that it travels at great speed when doing this. When it is lying partly outside its hole and finds itself observed, it withdraws slowly; but this withdrawal from sight is probably effected by pulling against the sides of its hole with its tail and therefore cannot be called swimming. Perch will sometimes take advantage of the help of an eel by following one that is digging in the bed of the river and snapping up such insects as may be disturbed. I tried to find the rate of growth of perch by cutting off part of their back fins and returning them to the water. I found that some quarter pound perch would almost double their weight in a year, whilst others only increased in size by a very small amount. At the close of a hot day during which no fish had fed and scarcely any had been seen, one sometimes saw deep down at the bottom of a pool flash after flash of silvery sides as the fish began to turn one after the other. They seemed to be rubbing their sides against the gravel and I imagined them as doing this in order to wake themselves after a long, lazy day, just as I rubbed my eyes when I awoke in the morning. The fish almost always fed freely just after doing this. Sometimes on a very hot day and in quite still water small roach would 'stand on their heads' in the water and remain motionless in this position for a long while; I always imagined that they had gone to sleep. In close, thundery weather the eels sometimes came to the surface and lay motionless beneath the water-lily leaves. A visitor captured quite a number with his landing net as Father pushed the punt along quietly by the lilies. During floods many fish left the river and came out over the grass. I often went along by the edge of the water with a dipper, sweeping it through the water and often throwing out small fish and eels. Chub would at such times go right out over the flood-ed meadows and could be seen swimming about with their back fins showing above the water. Chub, when lying on the surface of a pool, had two ways of retreating when alarmed. If one appeared suddenly, there was a tremendous swirl and the whole shoal went down at once; but, if they became uneasy but did not think they had been observed, they sank slow-ly in the water until they were out of sight.

One would not expect to find danger from the fish themselves when fishing in a quiet English stream. In the sea it would be different; there would always be the possibility of getting hold of a monster conger or even a shark. But I have on several occasions received severe stabs from the spines of perch, some of which swelled and became really painful. The spines on the gill-covers were more dangerous than those on the back, and one was much more likely to be injured by them since they were so much less conspicuous. I have also had several nasty bites from pike. One put its teeth right through one of my fingers and another stripped the flesh from the inside of a finger with the thick mat of teeth in the roof of its mouth. Another, from which I was trying to remove the hooks with my pocket knife, gave a sudden snap and swallowed the knife, which was not recov-ered until the fish was being prepared for cooking. I do not know if these attacks were intentional, or were merely automatic snaps against nothing in particular and that my hands happened to be in the line of fire.

Dragonflies

Chapter VIII

Insects

T has always seemed strange to me that, out of the thousands of different species of insects that surround us, very few people can recognise more than a dozen or two. Here and there one comes across a keen collector of butterflies and moths, more rarely a collector of beetles, and still more rarely someone who specialises in flies. I passed through the butterfly-collecting stage and for a time had jars covered with muslin in which I kept caterpillars and from which, in some cases, I hatched the perfect insects. But this happened after I had been to school for some time and had met other boys who were keen on forming collections. Before that time insects were creatures to be observed with interest, or passed by, just as the mood of the moment suggested. I very soon became familiar with a good many of the commoner kinds and those of outstanding appearance, or peculiar habits, naturally attracted attention; whereas inconspicuous insects, or those with nothing obviously curious about their habits, were almost ignored.

Almost the first insect to excite my curiosity was the house cricket, great numbers of which inhabited the cracks in the walls of the bakehouse around the great oven. The crickets were drawn to the bakehouse by the warmth there. They probably also fed on the flour; but this could not have been the main attraction, or they would have been equally plentiful in the mill. When the bakehouse had been unoccupied for an hour or two, the crickets would come to the edge of the crevices between the bricks and sit there 'chirping' so loudly that they could be heard quite clearly as one passed the door. There must have been hundreds of all sizes in the place. They seemed quite tame and, unless one made a sudden movement, would sit at the entrances of their homes and allow themselves to be watched closely. They were the only insects tolerated in any of the buildings, with the exception of the spiders which spun their webs from the rafters of the mill and were left undisturbed because they caught the flies and meal moths. Cockroaches came into the house kitchen, where they were trapped, and flies and wasps were trapped in the larder and dining room. The cockroaches, always referred to as 'black-beetles,' were trapped in a kind of metal pan into which they walked, but from which they could not escape. This was laid on the floor at night. I saw little of that, as it was set after I had retired to bed and removed before I got up. But the fly trap was a source of rather gruesome interest as it stood in the centre of the table. This trap was made of glass, shaped somewhat like a very broad-bottomed bottle, and was raised on little glass feet so that the flies could enter beneath and find their way to the channel of sugared liquid that ran around inside the bottom. In their attempts to drink the liquid, they lost their footing and soon drowned. The wasps were horrible in their dying struggles and would bite savagely at any fly that happened to be drowning near them.

In the garden there were several insects that drew attention to themselves by reason of their size, colouring or habits. Ladybirds were great favourites. We often caught these and handling them with great care, placed them on our hands and allowed them to climb up our raised fingers. As they did this, we would recite the following lines:

> 'Ladybird, ladybird, fly away home,
> Your house is on fire, your children are gone.
> All but one that lies under a stone.
> Fly away ladybird, fly away home.'

And almost invariably the ladybird raised its red wing-cases, stretched out its gauzy underwings and departed just as the last line was reached.

A snail was usually placed on the ground and threatened as follows:

> 'Snail, snail, come out of your hole;
> Or I will beat you as black as a coal.'

Whereupon the snail would thrust out its horns and head and proceed to crawl away.

Woodlice were found under stones and logs of wood. We called them 'chooky-pigs,' or 'Billy-buttons.' Their chief interest was their habit of rolling themselves up into a ball, so that they looked almost exactly like little lead bullets. Those found in the garden were chiefly dull lead-coloured, with an occasional sandy brown one; but up on the downs we found many that were darker in colour and shining like polished steel.

INSECTS

Garden spiders were liked because of their wonderful webs; but we always felt rather sorry for the poor flies which they captured, though we gloated over the struggles of the wasps as the spiders gradually wrapped them round and round with web till they had tied them in a tight bundle. We used to make the spiders 'dance' by touching them with a piece of grass; they would then shake themselves so violently that they disappeared in a sort of haze of movement. We were all afraid of the large spiders that sometimes came indoors in the summer; I still am. I was far more afraid of these creatures than I was of a rat. Some of the village people said that their bite was 'deadly poisonous'. They were supposed to be fond of music. Certainly they often hid behind the piano and came out when someone started playing and would sit on the wall as if listening. A very long-legged spider lived in the fields and several could always be found in the bed of a wagon that had just been unloaded at the rick. I was not afraid of these and sometimes caught one, but they had the most inconvenient habit of snapping off a leg or two directly they were handled. I did not like this and soon ceased to touch them. They were known as 'harvest men' and should not on this account be confused with the extremely minute red creatures which attacked us at harvest time and set up an intolerable irritation and which were called 'harvesters.'

On summer evenings chafers and great stag beetles often flew about the garden in such clouds that some collided and fell to the ground. I liked both these insects; but my sisters hated them because they sometimes became entangled in their long hair. The girls would rush screaming about the place because of the 'buzzy beetles'. There were two other interesting garden insects; one the humming-bird hawk-moth and the other the rose beetle. The hawk-moth flew swiftly over the flower beds, thrusting its long proboscis into each bloom. The rose beetles, which were not at all common, merely crawled; but they were attractive because of their lovely green colouring and because they were rare.

Dragon-flies were seen chiefly near the river. The village children were afraid of them, exclaiming 'they be stingers.' I never had any fear of them and did not believe them to be dangerous.

Probably Father had told me that they would not hurt me. I liked to watch them sail along at tremendous speed, sometimes shooting suddenly sideways and occasionally even flying backwards. They looked and behaved like insect hawks and were the only insects, except spiders, that seemed regularly to capture and devour other insects. Later on I found that there were many kinds of insect that preyed on other kinds.

Comma butterfly

Butterflies were numerous and varied; those best remembered being the brimstone, the meadow brown, the blues, the tortoiseshells, the peacocks and the red admirals. The brimstones were always the first butterflies to be seen in spring; the meadow browns were the commonest of all in the fields; the blues were the daintiest and seen throughout the summer in the lanes; the tortoiseshells always came indoors in the autumn and hung themselves up in some corner where they would remain throughout the winter, unless swept away by the turkey-feather brooms which were bought off the gypsies and used to sweep away cobwebs from high corners; the peacocks were not common and their lovely eyed wings always attracted attention; the red admirals were the latest and most lovely of all, they had a great liking for ripe pears and could always be seen in the top garden when the pears began to fall. Another favourite of the lanes was the orange tip. I remember seeing one year a great flock of clouded yellows on a clover field. Whites, of which I do not remember distinguishing the greater from the lesser, were so usual as to excite no interest. There must have been many more; but I do not remember anything about them. In the spring a clumsy, slow-moving, flat-footed, black beetle appeared in the hedges. When caught, it blew out of its mouth a bubble of reddish liquid resembling blood: hence its name, the Bloody-nose beetle. The large violet beetle was rather a favourite because of its graceful shape and deep-violet-coloured body. Scarlet soldier beetles were seen in scores on the heads of roadside flowers. Green tiger beetles raced about on hot, sunny days. At dusk the shining, blue-black door beetles went humming by and were often found upside down in the roads trying vainly to right themselves. I always thought that the numerous small parasites with which they were covered were their own young until I discovered that the fat 'bobs' I obtained for fishing from beneath cow pats were really the offspring of this beetle. In the quiet backwaters of the river one could always see companies of shining whirligig beetles skating rapidly about and running in to each other in the same stupid ways flies collide as they fly about the room. There were, of course, scores of others but they were just 'beetles.' Glowworms were scarcely ever seen near the farm; but on the rare occasions when we happened to be coming home after dark in summer, Father would often point out the soft greenish light in the roadside hedge.

Centipedes and millipedes were interesting because of their many legs; the latter, with their smooth, shining backs reminded me of slowworms, and the rippling movements of their many legs reminded me of the bending of cornstalks before a passing breeze. Caterpillars were rarely noticed unless they happened to be very brilliantly marked or curiously decorated; woolly bears were an exception and attracted notice by their habit of hurrying across the roads when searching for a place in which to pupate. The various looper caterpillars always drew attention to themselves by their curious method of walking; stretching forward to grasp with their front feet, then bringing their hind feet close up before again reaching forward to progress another half inch or so. The faces of grasshoppers reminded me of the faces of horses. Hoverer flies were 'darters,' because they darted off suddenly after hovering at one spot for a moment. An ant's nest had to be stirred with a stick, so that one might watch the excited insects rushing out to rescue their 'eggs.' Green-bottle flies sat in the sun on warm walls and doors; the ducks, which looked so clumsy, seemed to catch them with ease whenever they alighted within reach. Cuckoospits were uncovered whenever their bundles of white froth were discovered; but I did not then know that they were the same insects as the hard little froghoppers that jumped suddenly out of the grass and were so extremely hard to catch. Slugs were quite repugnant and have ever remained so, especially the very large ones. The brightly coloured shells of the hedge snails were much admired; I often brought home some of the prettiest. Some were bright yellow, others pink, some pink with broad chocolate-coloured bands. In a dry bank in one of the fields one could find scores of slender, pointed snail shells: but I never found one with a live snail in it. Humble bees were always called 'bumble bees.' This name seems more suggestive of the sound of their 'bumbling' flight. I was told that they did not sting, but found that they did, and pretty severely, if provoked. Wasps I was always afraid of and a 'wopse's nest' was carefully avoided. It was often dangerous to pass a wasp's nest in a roadside hedge, as the boys aggravated the creatures by pelting them with stones. The wasps would then attack anything that passed near the entrance to their nest. The blue-bag was always kept handy just inside the back door, so that this remedy could be applied directly anyone had been stung. Very occasionally a hornet appeared crawling up inside one of the windows. It was said that two hornets could kill a man and four a horse. I do not remember anyone being brave enough to kill one; but somehow or other they were coaxed out of the window as quickly as possible.

Sometimes pandemonium would reign amongst the horses. They would lay back their ears, kick-violently and refuse to move. The symptoms were always recognised at once. Someone would dart quickly under the horse, look on the inside of its thighs and give a quick slap. 'One o' they Forest flies. They diddykoi chaps brought 'en along, I reckon.' The Forest flies came from the New Forest, where the horses seemed immune, or at any rate indifferent to their attacks, and the gypsies coming from that direction sometimes brought one with them on one of their ponies. Our horses were not hardened to them and were driven frantic by their bites.

The worst fly attacking human beings was the rain fly. It was said to be a sure indication of rain in the near future when this fly began to make itself a nuisance. It was a greyish creature about twice the size of a house fly. It alighted so quietly that its presence was not suspected until it drove its 'stinger' into one's flesh. This sharp instrument, which it thrust from its mouth in order to make a hole in the skin through which to suck up blood, seemed to penetrate like a dagger and was extremely painful to children. 'Clegs,' as I now know them, do not bother me half as much as they used to; I can now endure the stab and so make a sure kill when the creature has comfortably settled down to its sanguinary feast.

I found water insects of particular interest and kept a good many in jam jars so that I could watch their habits. Water measurers were very fascinating as they skated about on the surface of the river, it seemed absurd to think that they were so light that their feet did not penetrate the surface film. I never saw a fish attempt to take one, though many years later I managed to delude a trout into snapping up one as I dropped it over a bush: but the trout made no attempt to take a second measurer presented in the same manner. I noticed that young domestic fowls would sometimes devour one of a certain species of caterpillar, but would refuse a second. No doubt many insects are very unpleasant to taste. Water boatmen were common in the shallow still parts. They came floating up to the surface tail first, remained suspended there for about two seconds, and then rowed themselves downwards again to the weeds and mud at the bottom. Sometimes I found a 'dragon' in a muddy backwater. This rather dreadful-looking creature turned out to be the young of the dragon-fly; so it seems I made rather a lucky shot in so naming it. There were often shiny black water beetles about half an inch long swimming amongst the weeds close to the edge of the river and sometimes in a meadow pond I found a specimen of the large dytiscus beetle, a creature of a rich brown colour with an outer edging of dull gold to the wing cases and almost as big over as a penny. Caddis worms in their cases were most interesting to watch and examine. The animals crawled about on the bed of the river or ditch, dragging their houses with them. When alarmed they withdrew indoors. Their houses, or cases, were made of a great variety of materials: gravel, bits of stick, weeds and often the shells of small water snails.

Weevils with their long snouts reminded me of elephants. Sometimes, by poking about amongst the rotting remains of a dead rat or bird. I came across one or two red-banded burying beetles. Skipjacks were very amusing; they always fell off the plant they were climbing when one disturbed them and landed on their backs. Then they doubled themselves into an arch and made quite a loud click as they bounded into the air and so regained their feet. The violet ground beetle was a large and very handsome creature. Green tiger beetles with yellow spots ran about the roads at a great pace and their bright colours always caught my eye. Sometimes under a piece of dead bark I found a beautiful little beetle, brilliant green beneath and with a green thorax; its wing-cases were a bright reddish colour. It (Chrysomela polita) was rounded like a ladybird and about twice that size. In the cob walls of one of the buildings at the dairy house were many small holes; I found that these were inhabited by a rather large and almost black bee.

Of course, it was necessary to study earthworms as they were required for fishing. The large, soft lobworms that come out of their holes at night were used for making eel clats; but were not a great success when used for

97

Comma butterfly

perch. The best perch worm was either a medium-sized, red worm known as a ' flat-tail,' or a tough, pale worm known as a 'blue-nose.' I have found since that our ' blue-nose' is known in some parts as a 'black-head.' I think our name is the best as its head, or 'nose,' is almost exactly the same tint as a human nose on a frosty morning. It is usually found in stony, clayey ground at the edges of roads. The bright red worm with yellow rings found in dung heaps I did not find of much use. Its strong smell was supposed to attract the fish; but it was very repulsive to human beings and I always believed it was the same to the fish. In damp spots beside the river and in almost any low-lying piece of ground one could sometimes find a green worm. These worms were small and nearly always found coiled in a couple of turns. They were not considered large enough for perch; but roach would often take them. They were, however, not sufficiently plentiful to be of much use as a regular bait.

I have already referred to the gnats that bothered us indoors at night in the summer; but to see gnats dancing in a sheltered corner of the garden on a winter's day was a gladdening sight as it was supposed to indicate the approach of more genial weather. Threads of spider web thrown across a path and catching in one's face, though unpleasant to feel, was always welcomed as a sign of a fine day to follow.

INSECTS

Long-waisted, active ichneumon flies, with brightly-coloured quivering bodies, running actively over the plants in the garden, were made even more interesting when one learnt that they laid their eggs in the caterpillars that frequently made such a mess of the cabbages and so disgusted one when they appeared amongst a portion of the vegetable on one's plate.

I often found little black insects creeping about the stems of plants and shrubs, particularly rose bushes. I called them 'crocodiles' and they certainly bore a slight resemblance to those creatures in the general shape of their bodies, though they were without any visible jaws. I found later from my books that these were young ladybirds. The lacewing fly was known as the 'fairy fly' which is quite a good name for this dainty, pretty creature. The weeds in the river abounded in small greenish leeches, which clung to one's legs when one paddled or bathed. At first I was afraid of them, as I had read about leeches sucking people's blood; but, when I found that these small creatures seemed incapable of breaking one's skin, I no longer feared them and found them interesting because of the extraordinary way they had of completely changing the shapes of their bodies. About the time the May trees flowered there would sometimes be a sudden appearance of great numbers of rather long-bodied, black flies which flew about in a stupid sort of way and were annoying because they sometimes blundered into one's face.

These creatures were lumped together as 'insects' and it was not until a good many years afterwards that I learnt to separate them into their proper groups.

'Elms beside the valley road.'

100

Chapter IX
Country Roads

HE Romans built roads 'as straight as a ramrod,' as they used to say when ramrods were in regular use in country houses in the days of muzzle-loading guns. Though I never saw a muzzle-loader used, one stood in the corner of the dairy and the beautifully embossed copper powder flask hung from a nail against the fire place on the wall of the dining room. There were the remains of a Roman road[5] on the downs and parts of several of the 'turnpike' roads were said to have been of Roman make originally. It was said almost as if it was an apology for their straightness; for no countryman seemed to like a long stretch of straight road. The distance seems longer when one can look down a road for nearly a mile and such a road is often very monotonous.

We rarely travelled on the turnpike roads, on some of which the old toll houses still stood with their windows facing up and down the road, so that approaching traffic could be seen from a distance; the doorway in the centre, from which the gate-keeper used to run to swing open the gate and take the toll. Our nearest route to the market town was by the valley road which curled along round easy corners and up and down little hills. I think I could still tell you every gate in that four and a half miles of quiet track and tell you an incident connected with every one of them, though it is now many years since I travelled it. This road, as well as all other roads as distinct from lanes in the district was surfaced with broken flints. The flints were brought and dumped beside the road where puddles after rain indicated that the surface needed repair. Then the flints in the heaps were broken into reasonably small pieces, generally by old men who sat there day after day wearing wire goggles and whacking away at the stones with a hammer; they were paid by the yard and, though the job was monotonous, it was a quiet and comfortable task for an old man on a sunny day.

---

5 Joyce is referring to the Roman road which ran past Badbury Rings from Lake Gates, west of Wimborne, where the Romans established a base camp for the conquest of south-west England.

Then the roadmen came with their barrows and shovels and spread the flints evenly over the road. When I was quite a small boy, these paths of flints were left rough and were hard to walk upon until the traffic had worked them in. They were also a trouble to the horses, for they often picked up a loose stone in their hooves. How often have I seen the pony suddenly begin to limp and heard Father exclaim, 'I think he has got a stone in his foot.' But every man who rode or drove a horse carried a knife to which was attached a hook specially designed to remove stones from the feet of horses; so the trouble was quickly remedied. Later on steam rollers were used to crush the flints into the road and the surface was rendered smooth in a much shorter space of time. These flint roads were at their best in winter, for even in the wettest weather they rarely became really muddy according to what was considered mud in those days. When a thaw came after a severe frost, little trickles of milk-like fluid ran across them when they lay over a chalk sub-soil. After a long spell of dry weather in summer the ground-up flints turned into fine dust mixed with tiny sharp splinters. The splinters were a great bother to the first users of pneumatic tyres and it was not at all unusual to get two or three punctures in the course of a ten-mile journey. The dust was often so deep that I have seen it trickling over the wheel-rim of a gig as it slowly climbed a steep hill. Swift traffic, or the passing of a large flock of sheep, sent it up in choking clouds so thick that one could scarcely see and leaving the hedges smothered in a film of grey. I have known a crop of clover quite ruined as horse fodder because of the amount of dust collected in it from a nearby road. On a windy day one's eyes and nose became filled with that dust that blew up in tormenting clouds. A green lane was then a real boon.

Nearly all our roads had a broad stretch of greensward running along on either side of the track. A cottager with a donkey would make sufficient hay from these green borders to keep his animals through the winter and some of those who kept one or two cows usually as a sideline to some village craft or trade, sent them out to graze along the roads under the charge of a boy. Since living in districts where roads have been cut right to the hedges I have come to realise what a great blessing these green verges are to the country walker. In some places there was a trotting track where riders turned their horses from the hard surface and allowed them to trot in comfort over the soft grass or beaten earth. In other places a pathway led up a slope until the foot-traveller could look down upon the vehicles passing beneath him. These raised pathways were always attractive to children and very few passed them without climbing up and enjoying the view from their elevated position.

COUNTRY ROADS

Traffic was mostly slow and comfortable. One neither dawdled nor hurried; but travelled at the pace of one's beast and enjoyed the scenery through which one passed. The modern low-seated car gives no idea of the real pleasure of country travel; one should be able to see over the hedges and move at such a pace that the objects passed are not merely just a scarcely recognisable blur. Here and there a real horse-lover possessed a fast-trotting cob behind which he rattled along at a spanking pace. Some of the more wealthy people drove a carriage and pair. When one of a pair had to be replaced, a good price could be made of an animal which exactly matched the horse that remained. Those who made driving a hobby sometimes turned out with a tandem; a footman rode behind and his services were sometimes required when the sudden appearance of a pig or a traction engine upset the nerves of the leader and made it turn round and face the wrong way. The horses of those days were much more nervous than they are now and the appearance of anything strange was enough to set the most staid of them capering; a traction engine was always a cause of anxiety to the driver. The law compelled the owner of a traction engine to have a man with a red flag walking a certain distance ahead of the machine. A local engine owner was fined because his man was a short distance under that prescribed in front of his engine. The next time the engine passed through the town, the man walked ahead with a tape measure attached to the front of the machine and his finger on the exact number of feet or yards required. Some considered this a piece of vulgar impertinence and an insult to the Bench; others looked upon it as a very good joke. Coaches, very much like the earlier stage coaches, travelled on pleasure trips between the principal towns. The driver sat on the box in front and controlled the four good trotters that drew the conveyance. At the back sat the man who blew the great copper horn as the coach approached a village or a corner. Some of these horsemen were proud of their skill and often blew a variation of a well-known tune as the coach came swinging up the street.

Bicycles were represented almost entirely by 'boneshakers' and 'penny-farthings,' and were chiefly used by workmen. The tyres were solid. A little later some of the older men took to tricycles; I expect their agility was no longer up to the standard required to manage the two-wheeled machines. A doctor and his wife used to ride out into the country on their tricycles. They were quite renowned locally on this account; the lady was considered very 'modern,' which was a polite way of indicating that her behaviour was not considered strictly correct.

All farm traffic was done by means of horses, with the exception of threshing machines which were drawn from one farm to another by the engine which also worked the machine when it reached the scene of its operations. The haulage of goods from the railway stations and ports was done by wagons and teams of stout farm horses. The carters took great pride in the appearance of teams when a journey had to be made outside their home district. Our wagons used to go every month or so to the nearest seaport and very smart they looked as they set out. Every inch of leather had been blackened and polished. The brasses, of which special sets were kept for these occasions, shone brightly. Bright ribbons fluttered from the manes and tails of the horses, plumes of white hair tossed above their shoulders and the leader carried a little peal of swinging bells. In summer each horse wore a clean pair of earcaps, decorated with tassels and blue and red braid. The paintwork of the wagon itself had been carefully washed and the clothes of the carter and his boy had been cleaned for the occasion. Even the special whip, a long whalebone affair with bands of brass at intervals along the handle, had been cleaned and polished. A well-got-up team was indeed a grand sight and I believe the true carter took a greater pride in his turn-out than in anything else with which he was connected. I do not remember ever hearing a grumble about the work this cleaning and decorating entailed; but I have heard the carters grumble at their stable boys for slovenly work. The horses themselves had been combed and brushed till they shone as brightly as polished wood; even their hooves had been greased and polished with the same care as the men had given to their own boots. I have never seen pride in the appearance of a machine such as the men had in the appearance of their wagons and horses.

I wonder if any specimens of the perambulators of those days have been preserved; I don't recollect seeing one in any museum. Shaped something like an easy chair and riding low upon wheels of wood, they were capable of holding two or three small children and a good many parcels. Perhaps they were designed for this purpose. One saw them chiefly on Saturday nights, when the workmen and their wives went to do the weekly shopping.

Usually the whole family went, because there was no one with whom to leave the children. Late at night one might see them returning; the foot of the perambulator loaded with parcels, perhaps three small children huddled together asleep on the single broad seat, another slightly older holding on to the handle to help its weary little legs along and the eldest trudging along beside his father. The journey alone, there and back, was probably nearly ten miles and on top of that these little children had to endure two or three hours crawling round the town after their mother. The men stood at the corners and talked with their friends, a few perhaps went into one of the public houses; but, though they might have a glass or two for company's sake, not many of the country working people drank to excess. Nine times out of ten the Saturday-night drunkard would be a townsman. An habitual drunkard in charge of horses would soon lose his job. The full-time shepherd was rarely seen in town, except on a Fair Day; sheep required daily and constant care and almost the whole of the shepherd's life and thoughts were taken up with them.

During ordinary times country roads were quiet and peaceful links between farms, villages and towns; but during parliamentary elections, and sometimes even during local elections, things livened up considerably. Every driver carried his colours attached to the top of his whip during an election; red or blue as the case might be, representing Liberal or Conservative. Feelings sometimes ran pretty high and it was no unusual thing for two particularly ardent but opposed drivers to slash at each other, or at each other's horses, as they passed. This sometimes led to a real set-to between men of violent dispositions. The opponents would descend from their respective vehicles, approach each other and indulge in abusive and often libellous back-chat. Then coats would come off and the matter would be settled with fists. Wise men kept their party feelings to themselves and, though they carried their colours as a matter of course, they did not respond nor retaliate when abuse was hurled at them or a whip fell upon their unfortunate horse.

Floods often caused trouble on the roads during winter. Sometimes a detour could be made through fields standing on higher ground; but I have often travelled some distance with my feet on the splashboard to keep them out of the water that ran through the bottom of the trap and once or twice I have seen the pony, so deep in the water that it probably had to swim for a few yards. Frost also hindered travelling by making the roads so slippery that the horses could not keep on their legs. The blacksmiths then had a busy time 'roughing' the horses' feet. This was done by drawing a few of the usual shoe-nails and substituting nails specially designed for the purpose with projecting heads which cut into the ice and enabled the horses to get a grip with their feet. A cow on an icy road was a pitiable object; its legs shot out sideways and the poor creature was soon sprawling on the ground.

The roads in many places had tall elms growing from the hedges. These trees looked very lovely during summer; but were often a trouble and danger during winter, when strong winds blew, particularly after much wet weather, some of these great trees came crashing across the roads and completely obstructed traffic. Often a journey would then be trebled in distance by reason of the detours that had to be made to get round these obstacles. I have known cases where the traveller became hemmed in on a stretch of road by trees that had fallen behind him during his journey, so that he could neither continue on his way because of an obstruction in front, nor return by, the same route by reason of another tree that had fallen across the road he had just travelled.

Though our country was a broad valley and therefore not so likely to be affected by deep snow drifts, there were occasions when road travelling was completely stopped for several days at any rate. In the downland country this was more frequently the case than with us, for the wind could there sweep unopposed over wide stretches of country, driving before it enormous masses of snow to be heaped up between the road hedges. A sudden fall and drift would sometimes catch the sheep on the exposed downs and bury them as they huddled for shelter in some hollow. During these times country people had to depend almost entirely on their own resources, as the usual services of butchers and bakers from the town could no longer reach them.

On Sundays we regularly drove to town in the 'fourwheeler' in the morning to attend service at the old Minster church[6]. Father went again in the evening, as he sang in the choir. I cannot remember being very entertained by the services; though I later discovered much beauty in the singing of the choir, which was of a very high standard. But I always thoroughly enjoyed the drive. It was my privilege to sit on the front seat beside Father and a drive with him through the country was never a dull affair. When he was not pointing out some interesting object, some unusual bird or some bit of local history, or even the beauty of an old half-timbered cottage, he would be singing to himself some beautiful selection from an Oratorio, or rehearsing the solo he would later render during the service. I have never progressed very far in musical knowledge; but those solos that Father sang as he drove along the road have always been my favourites and still bring a strange tingling thrill of happy memories whenever I hear them.

---

6 Wimborne Minster.

COUNTRY ROADS

Good driving is an art. They used to say that it was born in a man; if he had not 'good hands' a man would never be a good driver. Not one man in twelve ever reached the stage when he would be said to have 'good hands.' It was much the same with riding. A man could sit on a horse and even leap fences without falling off; but that did not make him a good rider. He had also to have 'good hands' and a 'good seat.' Such a rider seemed to be a part of the horse he rode. We saw them sometimes in the hunting field, but more particularly during the riding and jumping competitions at some country Fete or Horse Show. I had an uncle who had a great reputation as a driver. To sit beside him and travel swiftly along the roads in his little gig was a pleasure of a very definite quality. He always had the same type of pony and every one of them trotted the whole ten miles out from town to his farm without any change of pace and arrived in the yard apparently as fresh as when they started. He did not appear to exercise any control over the pony. The reins were held in the left hand and lay lightly along the pony's back, whilst his right hand rested most of the time on his thigh. Only when meeting or passing other traffic did the right hand touch the reins and then it seemed but the merest touch with the tips of the fingers. On the rare occasions when the pony failed to lift a foot high enough to miss a stray stone, the reins would be given a slight twitch and the animal reproved by voice. 'Come on now! Wake up there! What are you up to?' The pony would put back its ears, lift its feet and get back into its proper stride at once. It seemed so very easy, just as it looks so easy when you see a skilled musician playing on an instrument but the ordinary man could not do it like that.

Very few country people walked for the sake of walking; that was left to townspeople, who sometimes on a Sunday afternoon walked out to friends at a farm and stayed to tea. For any journey further than a mile a horse of some sort was used. If I was sent to the village, the centre of which was certainly not more than a mile from the farm, it was an understood thing that I should saddle the pony. The nearest farm could be reached in just over half a mile by taking a footpath through the fields; yet I never knew of anyone walking there, unless it happened to be one of the farm men in order to borrow a horse and cart to get on with some special job. This was not due to laziness, nor was it always due to a wish to save time; in some cases it certainly took longer to harness the pony and drive than it would have taken to walk the distance. I think it was custom more than anything else. Perhaps appearance also had something to do with it; it was certainly more imposing to drive up to a place than to walk there.

Mother, of course, always took out the pony and her own little two-wheeled trap whenever she wished to pay a call on friends. My cousins (they were really second cousins) and their father rode by every morning on their way to the Station to get the papers and always stopped for a few words with Father. They made a pleasant picture, the three boys and their father, each mounted on a well-bred and well-groomed horse.

Horse traffic on the roads drew many birds there, particularly in winter, to feed on the horse droppings. Rooks and jackdaws were the commonest scavengers to be seen there; but one saw a great many other birds besides. The powdered flints provided plenty of grit, of which all birds must have a constant supply. In dry weather also birds came there to dust. Small birds, such as finches and sparrows, could always be seen on a dry day scuffling in the loose places. Pigeons, partridges and pheasants, more particularly in the early mornings, were regular visitors. Some of the birds became so used to the horse traffic that they flew to the grass verges as one passed and returned again to their dusting or grit-pecking as soon as one had passed.

The times of the regular users of the roads were well known to most local people, so that it was not difficult to arrange to be at a certain spot at a certain time so as to be able to get a lift. This was never refused. Father never made any distinction with regard to the social standing of those to whom he gave a lift; he preserved the same kindly friendship towards everyone and I do not think there was anyone who ever said an ill word against him or even thought ill of him.

Between some of the villages and the towns there was a regular carrier's service. In some cases it was a daily service, in others only once or twice a week. This service was of very great use to many village people. By means of it they could send many goods to town and sometimes go to town themselves. The town tradesmen also made full use of it to send supplies to the small village shops and parcels of goods to country customers. It was slow, because it entailed a good many stops at various recognised points, and for this reason was sometimes a wearying journey for those who travelled by it. I expect many an old woman sighed in recollection of the days when she used to think nothing of tramping to town to do her shopping and got down wearily from the van where she had been sitting for perhaps two or three hours over a journey of five or six miles.

Country roads in my young days were much safer places for wild animals and birds than they are to-day. Nowadays it is no uncommon thing to find the corpses of four or five birds on a mile of road, particularly when

'Partridges uneasy'

the young birds are just beginning to fly. Only last autumn I came across the bodies of three hedgehogs that had been killed by cars within a distance of less than a mile. But it was easy for the wild things to get out of the way of the horsedrawn vehicles. I remember seeing Father catch a partridge in rather a curious way. We were driving along the valley road and presently saw two partridges engaged in a terrific battle some distance ahead. Father withdrew the whip from its socket and held it ready. As we approached, one bird flew off; but the other ran along on the grass verge. Father flicked at it with the whip, the thong caught round its neck and he drew it up into the trap and killed it. We then saw that this bird had lost the whole of the skin from the back of its skull. I do not know if this had been done by its opponent; or if it had been struck and injured previously, perhaps by a hawk. Wild creatures frequently attack any of their own species that have met with an injury. Domestic animals often do the same. I once saw a herd of cattle horning one of their companions to death. No doubt the unfortunate beast had received some severe injury and so had incited the others to attack it. On another occasion a cow, which I had helped rescue from a ditch, was pushed into another ditch by its companions the very next day and drowned. This instinct, though apparently so cruel, no doubt serves a very useful purpose under natural circumstances. A herd with one of its members wounded would certainly attract the attention of any carnivorous beast in the neighbourhood.

People in cars nowadays resent sheep on the roads because they have to reduce their speed almost to walking pace in order to get past these rather stupid creatures. In the old days one didn't mind having to pull aside in the slower horse-drawn trap or carriage when one met a flock of sheep; but, should it be summer time and in a dry spell, they caused a very real inconvenience through the clouds of dirt they stirred up. The coming of a flock would often be heralded by the sight of this pall of dust hanging over the road in the distance. Two thousand sharp little feet can kick up a great deal of choking dust on a dry flinty road. Pigs were more dangerous, because they had an objectionable habit of suddenly running across a road in front of a horse. One of our best driving horses was thrown and injured by a pig running across the road in front of it. When acorns were plentiful great droves of pigs were sometimes seen on the roads in charge of small boys. Sometimes a donkey or a goat would be tethered beside the road. Occasionally a travelling herd of goats came into the district. We were told that they came from Wales. The drovers tried to sell from their flock as they travelled through the country. When cattle had been bought at one of the regular auctions, they were driven to the farm of the purchaser by recognised cattle-drovers who attended the sales and cattle auctions, or Repositories as the latter were sometimes called. These men often had considerable difficulty in getting their charges through the journey, as the animals got frightened in a strange district and often tried to break back towards their old homes. Circuses had the roads almost to themselves as they travelled chiefly at night. Their goods were all horse-drawn and they presented a tremendous cavalcade, some of the larger circuses having nearly fifty horses in their outfit. Cyclists, except for the local men on their penny-farthings, were a rare sight; but, considering the roughness of the roads, it was amazing the distances some of those early cyclists travelled. I once saw two young men at the farm at mid-day who had ridden that morning from London, a distance of one hundred and ten miles. Their machines had cushion tyres. I should not care to attempt such a journey on pneumatic tyres even on the modern smooth-surfaced roads.

There was a quietness about country roads when I was a child which I miss now. Most of the traffic consisted of farm vehicles and the majority of these moved quietly and slowly because of their loads.

The fastest vehicle on the roads was a gig, with a smart horse in the shafts; the noisiest was the traction engine. In fine weather we went for a walk every afternoon and usually chose the lanes. Nearly all the lanes had sheep tracks along the wide grass verges and these we always preferred to the metalled surface of the main track. There was adventure, also, in these little sheep tracks. They went up and down, and twisted slightly in their courses; the hard main track was much more level and kept to a straight course which tended to become monotonous. There were also the sur-face-water catch-pits, cut deeply into the verges at right angles to the road, and all of these had to be jumped. After a heavy shower they might hold six inches of water and to leap from one high mound to the other required considerable nerve. The gutters themselves would be attractive when filled with dead leaves in autumn; it was delightful to wade through these and feel them billowing about one's legs, but the only time when the road itself was really attractive to walk upon was when it was deep in dust, scuf-fling through which also was a great pleasure even if it did bring a sharp reprimand. In addition what roadside hedges are so filled with flowers as those in chalk country!

Perch fishing

Chapter X

Country Amusements

INCE travelling in the country was a somewhat slow process and depended almost entirely upon the horses available, amusements were in the main confined to such things as the immediate neighbourhood provided. Those who hunted travelled further afield; but the followers of hunting were chiefly drawn from well-to-do private individuals and farmers who could afford to keep hunters in addition to their working horses. There were, of course, amusements that formed a regular part of the farm routine; such, for instance, as rabbiting and ratting. Though both these animals had to be destroyed, or at any rate, kept within bounds, for the sale of the crops, their destruction was always so organised as to fulfil some kind of sporting requirement. Then an assault upon the rats was usually made the occasion for the entertainment of some sport-loving friend who happened to possess a good ratting terrier; and one or two days were set aside every winter for the purpose of getting together a small shooting party and making a serious attack upon the rabbits.

Father's love of music and the river close at hand naturally made music and fishing the chief amusements in which we took part. The first was confined mostly to the winter months, when people with similar tastes would arrange musical-evenings at each others' houses in turn for the purpose of rehearsing vocal solos, duets, quartets and instrumental items in preparation for the annual concert held in every village. The second was spread over the whole year; a day or two after perch in summer and a day or two after pike in winter being regular features.

Father's singing took him to every village and town within a ten-mile radius and sometimes even further. For many years I do not think there was a concert within reach of horse conveyance at which he did not assist. His regular partner was a chemist who had a business in the market town[7] and who was an excellent comic. With these two names on the bill any concert

---

7 Wimborne Minster.

was assured of a full house. Father's contribution was always a selection of really high-class ballads, all of which were most carefully rehearsed and sung with genuine feeling. I have never heard him sing at a concert without getting an encore and often a double encore. The chemist was equally conscientious in his work, nor did he ever allow any vulgarity to creep in. In those days any looseness of speech, whether in public or private, was severely frowned upon and those who transgressed could rest assured that they would not be welcome in any respectable society. Occasionally some performer with a town reputation would be introduced as a novelty in village pantomime but, should he happen to be one who relied on getting a laugh from the back seats of the hall at his doubtful jokes, he would find that the organisers, who always sat somewhere towards the front, forgot him the next time a concert was being arranged. Some said that the chemist would have made a name for himself if he had gone on the professional stage; but others, who regarded the professional actor, with the exception of the recognised leaders, as of very doubtful moral worth, stated that he was too good for that sort of thing. Father, when singing at a concert in a fashionable seaside town, was approached to join the Covent Garden chorus. He was then a young unmarried man and his parents would not consent.

The village concerts were really great fun; friends met and chatted together as they came in, for everyone from the surrounding district attended. The schoolroom was the usual place at which all village meetings were held; often it was the only place available. Before the performance started there was a continual rustling of skirts and scraping of chairs as the earlier arrivals turned to check in those coming later. At the back, admitted for a penny or twopence, were the farm labourers, gardeners, coachmen and local artisans, usually accompanied by their wives and often their children. Probably the vicar opened the proceedings with a short speech of welcome and a description of the objects of the entertainment and details of the fund that was to benefit. If possible the first item would be a pianoforte duet, if a duet pair could not be found, there would be a pianoforte solo. Then followed a varied assortment of songs, recitations and instrumental music; great care being taken to see that the item following a comic number was not one that would be too much overshadowed by the general appeal of the comic. Sometimes monologues, duologues or even One Act Plays helped out the performance. Plays were without exception either comedies or farces, the latter for preference. I never once saw a serious attempt at straight acting in any of these concerts. One extremely popular item was an absurd story describing how someone, having made some cherry brandy, threw the cherry-pulp out into the yard, where it was eaten by the geese. The geese became intoxicated and were thought to be dead. In order that they should not become a total loss to their owner, they were plucked for the sake of their feathers. The chill of their nakedness eventually roused the geese from their stupor and they were seen walking about the yard in this sad condition. To make them comfortable until their feathers should again appear, the farmer's wife made them waistcoats of red flannel. It was the sight of these birds going about in their red garments that invited a question and introduced the story. I must have heard that recited at least half a dozen times. Occasionally the concert was followed by a dance, the dancers being drawn chiefly from the front seats. Dancing in those days was almost entirely confined to the members of the upper and middle classes. A definite class distinction pervaded the whole of society and not only were certain amusements confined almost entirely to certain classes, but the members of the respective classes for the greater part only partnered others from their own class, or even their own set, in their amusements. Even in these small village dances the proceedings were conducted with the usual decorum. A man did not dance with a girl without first obtaining an introduction, either or by the M.C.,[8] or by some intimate friend or relative, and a request as always accompanied by a graceful bow. Dances in those days were strenuous affairs, the programme consisting chiefly of polkas, schottisches, waltzes, quadrilles and lancers.

Father usually arranged several fishing outings during the year; a lovely lazy day or so in summer, gliding quietly along in the punt and tying up beneath the shade of a willow to fish for perch; or a more strenuous day in overcoats and thick boots during winter after pike. Most of these outings were arranged for the benefit of an angling friend from town; few country men indulged in any serious angling, though one of our most regular and welcome winter visitors was a retired farmer. I sometimes fished with the summer parties and in winter I could always make myself useful, and so watch the sport, by carrying the can of live bait. The landowner across the river was a very keen pike angler and came down several times every winter with a party of friends. I was generally allowed to go with them and was sometimes given a fish and the remains of the live bait at the end of the day. The live bait were put in eel box, a box with holes in it which was tied to a stake and sunk in the river and in which odd eels were kept alive until sufficient had been caught to make a meal. Later on, when I had an hour or two

---

8 Master of Ceremonies, or compere.

'The peewit's love flight.'

to spare, I would take one or two of these bait and go after pike myself. One member of this landowner's party was an excitable Frenchman named Souberbielle who resided in the district and was known to the village people as Mr. Sober-Billy. It was an amazing and amusing sight to see his antics when he hooked a good-sized pike. He would dash up and down the bank, shouting for the gaff and exclaiming 'I vill let him go! I vill let him go!' Then, when the fish at last had been safely landed, he would strut about with pride, and with much gesticulation and exaggeration, go over the details of the exciting battle. He was the only Frenchman I had ever met and I thought they must be a very remarkable race if they all resembled him.

I never once saw a country workman fishing with hook and line. He could not very well have done so as there was no water available for him except the pools under the bridge. By custom it was agreed that an angler could fish from any bridge crossed by a public road. The village men and farm hands went to the bridge for the purpose of snaring pike, at which practice they were very skilled. A long pole, with a stout cord and wire snare attached was always kept under the roof of our cart-horse stable ready for anyone who happened to spot a pike lying within reach from the bridge. Often a workman on his way home across the bridge would look over and see a pike. Then he would come running into the stable. 'Can I borry the jack pole?' he would say to the carter, or whoever happened to be about. Then the two would hurry off to the bridge and for perhaps twenty minutes you might see them carefully trying to get the noose over

Peewit chick

the pike's head without alarming it. The village men were allowed to go 'clodding' for eels anywhere and by this means often supplied their families with a change of diet.

Rabbiting meant either ferreting or shooting over dogs. When the ferret was used, one might either bolt the rabbits into nets, or shoot them; sometimes, when one gun only was available, both methods were employed at the same time, the gun attending to one side of the hedge, the man working the ferrets having nets on his side. When using a ferret the greatest care was taken that there should be no unnecessary noise; no loud talking or stamping about. A good ferreter scarcely ever spoke above a whisper and moved as softly as a cat. Often the only intimation the gun would have that a rabbit had bolted on the other side of the hedge was the dead rabbit held up for him to see and a cautionary silent signal that another had been heard moving inside the bury. He also handled the ferret quietly and kindly, so that it should not be made nervous and difficult to catch. Boxing Day was the great day for a party to shoot rabbits over dogs. Arrangements to provide a sufficient number of beaters, guns and dogs were made well beforehand. A start was usually made at ten o'clock in the morning. Allowing for a break of about an hour at mid-day for lunch, this made a day of about five hours for shooting, which was quite as much as most of the dogs could stand. The farm hands were given a holiday and, clad in stout leggings and with folded sacks tied over their knees and thighs, they entered the gorse and brambles and spent a thoroughly enjoyable day helping the dogs drive the rabbits out to the waiting guns. They were as keen as anyone and worked as hard, or harder, than any day in the fields. Their excitement was tremendous and very few rabbits succeeded in breaking through their lines. Their reward was a free and liberal lunch and a couple of rabbits to take home. Anyone bringing along a useful dog was allowed an extra rabbit as the dog's reward.

When rats were the quarry, guns were left at home and stout sticks took their place. Two people with a dog apiece and two or three ferrets could very well manage the banks. If rats were very plentiful it was sometimes advisable to double the number of men and dogs, but it could easily be over-done. One good dog on either side of the bank would do as well as two in most cases. Dogs that were strangers to each other were liable to become jealous. They were naturally in a highly excitable and even savage state when tackling rats and a dog-fight did not help matters in any way. There was also a danger that the over-eagerness due to the presence of a rival might make them in rather too much of a hurry to get at anything moving and a valuable ferret might get snapped up in the heat of the moment. Too many people often got in each other's way and over excitement here some-times resulted in a dog getting a whack instead of a rat. A rat that had escaped dogs and sticks and regained the bank often refused to bolt again and would stand and fight the ferret; so would an old doe rat with a nest of young. Ferrets could usually look after themselves; but occasionally one got badly bitten and would come out eventually with its lovely white coat red with blood. I have never seen a ferret killed by a rat; but I have often known one get a badly festering wound from a rat's bite. A professional rat-catcher was very clever in dealing with rats which refused to bolt. Most of these turned at bay close to the entrance to the bury. As soon as the rat-catcher saw one sitting with its back to the opening of the hole, he would slip in his hand, grab the rat by the tail, whip it out and under his left armpit in one movement, then, changing his grip to the animal's shoulder as he held it pressed against his side, he would place its head in his mouth, give it a quick bite and throw the dead rat down. I certainly could never put any part of such a filthy creature as a rat in my mouth; but I adopted the first part of his method of capture and, having drawn the rat out by the tail, in one swift movement I would swing it round my head and bring it down across my boot, or on to the ground with all my force. I have killed scores of rats in this way and, if one of the workmen was present, felt flattered by his praise of my quickness and courage. I think I can count myself extremely lucky that I was never bitten; though the whole thing depends on quickness throughout the action, as a rat cannot very well turn on its own tail.

COUNTRY AMUSEMENTS

My hunting, and hunting always referred to foxhunting, consisted of little more than going to an occasional meet and following the hunt for some distance on foot. Sometimes the distance covered by this method was tremendous: I found by checking up one run on the map that I had covered thirty-five miles from home to my return home some time after dark. I was never much of a horseman; besides which, we had nothing suitable for me to ride. The pony which Mother drove would certainly have saved my legs; but, as I should have had to go alone, I was much too afraid of looking ridiculous by falling off, or doing something equally silly, that I would not make the attempt. This nervousness in public held me back in a great many things, even in shooting; I had shot my first snipe before I could be persuaded to bring my gun to a shooting party. I well remember the occasion when first I shot with others. I had turned up with my dog and stick as usual and had worked hard all the morning as a beater. One of the guns was the retired farmer who used to come pike fishing in winter. During the halt for lunch he asked if I did any shooting and Father told him that I seemed to be getting pretty good at it. I was then asked why I did not bring my gun to the shooting parties and again Father had to speak for me and said that I seemed to be afraid I should not be able to shoot with people looking on. At one of the beats after lunch the retired farmer was posted at a quiet corner of the copse we were beating and, seeing me near, called me over and persuaded me to take his gun. I was not nervous in his presence, as I had spent many days with him by the river. I shot well and got every rabbit that tried to cross the drive. Old Jack praised me up to the skies when the drive was over and made me take his gun for the rest of the day. That broke the ice and though I was often too nervous to shoot at my best in company, I never again refused to make one of the guns at a party. Father, when a small boy, used to go hunting on a donkey; but I don't suppose he ever got much further than the meet. I never once knew the hounds to run a fox within sight of the farm; nor have I ever seen them draw any of the fields or withy beds nearby.

The best place from which to view the hunt was from the highest rampart of the old 'Roman' camp up[9] on the downs. One could spend the whole day walking around the rampart and with any reasonable degree of luck have the hunt in view nearly the whole time. Sometimes the fox would be found amongst the brambles and gorse in the centre of the camp itself and, if not at home there, it was almost certain to be found in one of the two

---

9 Badbury Rings, an Iron Age hillfort.

Owl being mobbed

woods close by – the High Wood and a lower wood of very ancient oak trees known as The Oaks. All the farmers were keen on hunting, even those who never rode to hounds themselves, and not one of them would kill a fox or allow a fox to be killed, except by the recognised method of hunting. To be able to produce a fox when hounds met in the vicinity was every farmer's pride. A litter of cubs on a farm was a thing to boast about and visitors on a summer evening were handed the field glasses and taken by a carefully-chosen route to some hedge from behind the shelter of which they might watch the pretty little creatures romping and tumbling before the mouth of their home. Anyone who even spoke against a fox was looked upon as ignorant, prejudiced and an enemy to the State. A fox-hater was regarded as something little short of a criminal.

An attempt was once made to hunt the otter. The pack had no difficulty in finding its quarry; but the river was too deep for the hounds to keep in touch with the otter. I believe two or three otters were found that day; but in each case the hunt lasted only a few minutes. The attempt was not made again.

From time to time a coursing meeting was arranged by the farmers, when the quarry was the hare. The meeting was an invitation affair and confined to personal friends. One or two of the farmers kept a greyhound, or perhaps a pair, and selected friends were asked to bring theirs so as to have a competition between the animals. Our hares were big and strong and it took an exceptionally good pair of dogs to catch one once it had got on to the open downland. A hare put up from stiff plough-land was almost sure to be caught, unless it could get on to grass or stubble. It was astonishing to see what a difference this made to the speed of the animal. A hare might be doubling only a yard or two in front of the dogs on the heavy ploughland and its end seemed only a matter of seconds; then by clever turning it would get to a 'Mesh' (the 'mesh' or opening in a hedge through which hares pass from one field to another), and slip through on to the grass. A couple of seconds advantage as the dogs got through the hedge and the next moment you would see the hare going straight away towards the skyline with the hounds completely outdistanced. Most of the hounds were really faster than the hare over a short distance; but they could not keep up the pace for so long and their weight carried them beyond their quarry when the hare made a quick turn almost under their jaws. A good pair of hounds would work together, neither of them running straight at the hare, but each keeping slightly to one side or other of the hare's line. Then, as they drew close, one greyhound would dart in from its side and the hare would turn quickly, only to find itself confronted by the other dog. A few more turns like this and one or other of the dogs was able to make its kill. A hare was always given good 'law' before the hounds were slipped. A slipper who allowed a hare to be chopped, by not giving it sufficient start before releasing the hounds, was soon removed from his post. A hare that made good its escape after a hard run was always well praised. I think every one admires speed in an animal and I know of nothing that gives so vivid an idea of amazingly rapid animal movement as the close-passing of a hunted hare with the greyhounds straining behind it. In these terrific bursts of speed both animals reach forward with their hind feet far in front of their forefeet and cover tremendous distances at each bound. Sometimes it is the hound that is killed in coursing; I once saw a greyhound break its neck by running into a hedge-bank when it overshot the hare it was chasing. It was killed instantly. These coursing meetings were always perfectly straight sporting affairs. There were no bookies or other followers. Any betting that might be done was just a friendly affair between the owners of the dogs, and the onlookers consisted solely of the farmers and their personal friends. When hares got very numerous it sometimes became necessary to organise drives in order to reduce their numbers. These drives, were more in the nature of farming than sporting meetings. A driven hare is an easy target, the only difficulty being to organise the drive so that a sufficient number of hares go forward, to face the guns. This is not at all an easy matter. In some uncanny way the hares often seem to know that danger awaits them half a mile ahead behind the hedge and all the shouting and waving of arms by the drivers will not prevent a good many breaking back through the line of safety. A gun or two with the line helped to send the hares forward; but that often meant that the guns in front were too wide apart, or the flanks had to be left unguarded. I have often seen twenty hares started in the course of a drive; yet the bag might be no more than five.

A coot drive was another winter amusement. To arrange this it was necessary to get into touch with all the farmers who had meadows bordering the river; which could generally be managed when all met on Market Day in the town. A suitable day for all having been selected, the time was then arranged at which the guns would be ready in their respective places along the river. The farmer on the lowest stretch had simply to go to his bottom boundary and walk up the river bank until he came to the next gun. The second gun would then walk up to the next and so on. At the conclusion of the drive the two ends of the line usually walked up or down stream, as the case might be, so that all would meet at a central point to compare notes, share out the spoil and perhaps partake of some refreshment. A few duck and teal generally managed to find their way into the bag on these actions.

Though women often hunted and some joined the outings after perch and gudgeon in summer, very few were ever seen in the shooting field. Sometimes a few ladies were seen at the coursing meetings; they were mostly dog-lovers who had themselves taken a good part in exercising the greyhounds. But women's open-air amusements were chiefly confined to croquet and tea parties. It would be a mistake to suppose that their lives were dull in consequence of this absence of outdoor amusements. The majority of women took a very real interest in the management of their homes and the upbringing of their children, and matters connected to these subjects formed an endless source of interested conversation. Most educated women, also, were skilled in some form of art. Drawing, painting and music had formed an essential part of their education and the results were displayed in the decoration of their homes and the entertainment of their friends. Fancy needlework of many kinds had many ardent followers and the product of their industry was displayed in the multitude of curtains, cushions, valances and table mats with which their houses were filled. Deportment also was a subject requiring constant and unflagging attention. Under no circumstances would any self-respecting woman forget her man-

Dabchick

ners. Many took a great interest in the work of the village church. As host-esses at the many little parties, whether for adults or for children, women had plenty of scope for the exercise of their organising abilities and oppor-tunities for displaying the completeness of their domestic arrangements and the correctness of their behaviour in public and before guests. There were usually two Balls held every winter in one or other, and sometimes in both, of the nearest market towns[10] and at these the ladies had every reason to consider themselves as the most important members of the company. One of these Balls was organised by the Yeomanry, the other by the Hunt. The latter had perhaps the highest social standing; but the Yeomanry, consisting as it did in those days almost entirely of farmers and landed gentry, drew a following almost as well leavened with the 'County' as did the function organised by the Hunt Committee.

A good many women were skilled card players; but card playing amongst women was not general in country society. The men, after a day's shooting, might sit down to a game of cards' with their whisky; but any ladies of the party would usually be found sitting in the drawing room. Drawing rooms were, by the way, rarely entered except when guests were present; for the rest of the time the contents were shrouded in dust sheets and on opening the door of one of these rooms a curious and distinctive

---

10 Wimborne Minster and Blandford Forum.

musty smell met one's nostrils. A 'drawing room' smell was a regular term amongst us children in describing anything that smelt musty. We rarely saw cards in our home; music took up most of the time available for indoor recreation by adults.

Nearly every farmer in our district kept one or two terriers. Most of these were excellent ratters and would go through the thickest cover for rabbits. Very few spaniels were kept. One farmer, who did a good deal of partridge shooting, had a pair of clumbers; these were considered rather exceptional dogs, as they would both hunt and retrieve. They were slow and felt the heat very much in warm weather when working thick gorse; but they were very reliable and persistent. These small hunting dogs were all docked. This was a necessary precaution against injury to their tails and had nothing to do with giving them a smart appearance. When hunting and on a hot scent, the dogs thrashed their tails vigorously and a dog with a long tail would soon have had it badly torn. I knew of two injuries as the result of tails not being docked as a puppy. One had to be docked later in life owing to festering from scratches by thorns. The other had been left with rather too much tail and the tip soon got badly torn. The pain it suffered caused it to gnaw its tail after a day's hunting. Eventually it removed the offending point and had no further trouble. We were always rather sorry for poor old Pincher as he lay snarling and gnawing at his own tail and were quite glad when he got rid of the constantly raw tip. There was one quite useful terrier which was a regular member of our hunting parties and which had an undocked tail which seemed to cause it no trouble; but I noticed that this dog, which was rather a long legged animal, never pushed under the thick stuff in the way the shorter legged dogs did. It had a smooth coat and this and its long tail possibly taught it to go carefully when it came to a particularly stiff bit of cover, under which it would have found it difficult to scramble by reason of its long legs. Docking was performed in rather a crude fashion; but I do not think the operation caused very much pain. It was done when the puppies were quite small, sometimes with a chopper and block, a hammer being employed in order to ensure that the cut was made exactly at a joint; but experts preferred to bite off the unwanted portion. Bleeding was stopped by means of a dab of cobweb pulled from under the thatch of some shed. Though this sounds very insanitary, I never saw any ill results. If one could judge fairly by the noise made, the puppies were not hurt nearly so badly as the young pigs when the latter were 'ringed' and castrated. The ringing, carried out in order to prevent the pigs rooting up everything, including probably the posts of their own sties, was a dreadful business; castration seemed much less painful. The whole time it was in progress the air was filled with the most terrible squealings. I hated to hear the pigs squealing in pain, though many of the squeals were only sympathetic; when one little pig started to shout, all the others joined in. The squealing at feeding times was quite different and had rather a jolly sound about it.

Having been brought up with country sports as part of natural surroundings, it has almost naturally followed that they have continued to be a source of very great pleasure to me, but I have always been very glad that the attitude of those with whom I was connected, when first I was brought into touch with such things was that the first principle of any sport should be that the game pursued be given the fullest reasonable chance of making its escape. Whether the sport was hunting, shooting or fishing, I was made to understand that it was not the bag which counted so much as the manner in which the bag was obtained. Most field sports on a farm are, to a certain extent, an essential part of the work of the farm; but this does not mean that, though rabbits, for instance, must be kept down, any manner of reducing their numbers, is justified. So it follows that, though hunting, shooting and fishing have always been almost a part of my nature, the pleasure I have found in them has been in my own, or others' skill, pitted against the cunning, speed or wariness of the creature pursued. Big bags have, in fact, always been repugnant to me and memories, even of my earliest adventures, have always been most vividly retained in connection with those incidents where particularly exacting circumstances formed an essential feature; a really clever stalk, a shot taken after a prolonged hunt or under very difficult conditions; or a large and wary fish taken on light tackle after a long and trying battle. Though Father shot snipe on the ground, because he couldn't hit them flying and because Mother considered them such dainties, he frowned upon any pot-shots taken through the hedge and was delighted when he saw me bring off a really good kill.

'Watering circus ponies'

126

Chapter XI
Village Amusements

HERE seems to be this great difference between the modern working man and the working man of my childhood, at any rate as regards those who lived in the country. Nowadays one sees men, particularly young men, cycling into the towns after their day's work for an evening's amusement and this amusement consists chiefly in getting someone else to amuse them. 'The Pictures' are, of course, the great draw and in the main I believe this to be good; they are a form of education and must considerably brighten the lives of the country working people. But in the days of my childhood there were very few entertainments provided, even in the towns. The lads and men of the villages had to provide their own amusements, with the result that nearly everyone of them had some craft or hobby in which he might really be considered somewhat of an expert. Most of the men were skilled gardeners and took great pride in the produce of their gardens. In nearly every village there was a band and, although the same tunes could be heard from all of them, these village bands were often excellent. They formed a very useful part of almost every sort of public function. When the 'Foresters' paraded for church on 'Whit Monday' morning, the village band led the way and played again in the afternoon at the Fete that was always held on that day. The band also played at the annual Flower Show and at Christmas time they usually turned out to give Carol selections. At one time, no doubt, they assisted at the May-Day revels; but these had ceased when I was a boy, though I believe Maypole dancing has been revived by the school children and now forms a regular May-Day feature. Many of the young men played mouth-organs and concertinas. Their playing was done entirely by ear and the style was distinctive, the same sort of rhythm creeping into every tune. The mouth-organ, being such a small instrument, could be carried in the pocket and it was common enough to hear one being played as a young man passed along the road at night, perhaps after spending an hour or two with some 'maid' of his choice, 'maid' being the term quite properly applied to any unmarried girl and not necessarily referring to one in domestic service as it now so often does.

The older men often played quoits or skittles. Most of the public houses had some sort of a skittle alley and there was often a paddock at the back where the men could throw their quoits and sit on a bench under a tree with a drink beside them.

Nearly every village had its cricket team; but the game, being so strictly limited in the number of its players, was for most of the men an interesting spectacle rather than something in which they could take an active part. Our village cricket pitch was at the back of the vicarage. The vicar was a very keen supporter of the team and, with a view of encouraging hard hitting, willingly paid a shilling to anyone who could break a window in the vicarage by a full boundary hit. It required some luck and a mighty good swipe to do this; I saw it happen once only. A vigorous hitter was always popular. 'Let drave at 'em' the old men under the chestnut tree would shout as some sturdy favourite went to the wicket. His life was often short; but there was plenty of 'dravin', whilst he remained in. Energy was preferred to style and, though he might step out once too often and lose his bails before he could get back to his crease, his ten or a dozen mighty slogs had added a few runs to the score of his side and earned him loud applause from his supporters. I have noticed that nearly all the village youths used to blush as they came off the field and heard the clapping and shouts from their friends. Sometimes there would be a holiday schoolboy in the team, home from 'college' - according to the villagers everyone who went away to school went to college. The schoolboy usually had style and confidence. He was generally bowled by a ball that fitted into no style and his expression was often one of annoyance as he came off the field. I preferred the modest blush and obvious delight in his performance shown by the village lad; in fact, I preferred village cricket, with its tip-and-run speed, to the more correct style and rather wearisome length of the game as played by the town teams.

The girls played hop-scotch with a flat stone on a pitch scratched out in the dust of the road. The boys played marbles against a handy wall; or tip-cat in a good open space, this game being too dangerous to windows to be tolerated near dwelling houses. 'Konkers' also had their short season when the horse chestnuts began to fall. Rounders was often played in a field on a summer evening. But there was no regular play time for the village children: such time as they had for games was taken in odd moments between jobs. Sometimes the boys got occasional jobs, when they were not at school, 'bird starving,' looking after pigs turned out in the barley stubble after harvest, pulling docks or cutting thistles; the girls had plenty to do helping their mothers or looking after the younger children, and nearly all of them went 'out to service' as soon as they were old enough, which was when they reached fourteen or fifteen years of age. I do not think that the children were any the less happy by reason of not having any regular play hours; they were nearly always occupied and children who are occupied are nearly always happy.

Though boys and girls of school age played games together to a certain extent. I do not remember ever seeing the young men and women playing any kind of organised mixed games. A fellow was said to be 'playing games with a girl' when he took part in the usual mild horseplay that went on at every open-air gathering at which both parties met. The sexes kept together in little companies of twos and threes, as if for protection against the other sex. The lads were somewhat the bolder, at any rate outwardly. It was one of them who would step up behind the selected girl and tickle her under the ear with a blade of grass. After two or three of these playful assaults, the girl usually rose to the bait and chased the fellow for perhaps ten yards before returning blushing to her companions. These antics were, as everyone knew, merely the preliminaries to lovemaking. I used to think how closely they resembled the antics of a couple of cats under similar circumstances. The next step in their love-making would be 'walking out,' then would follow 'arming' and, when it got to that stage, the 'intentions' were so obvious that he would be recognised as her 'young man' and she as his 'maid,' the expressions in both cases having the word 'affianced' understood. In no walk of life was there the free mixing of the sexes amongst young people that is usual nowadays; even tennis, a rather feeble exhibition of pat-ball in which a man was considered anything but a gentleman if he returned a ball hard at a woman opponent, parents and elders sat around the lawn and kept a watchful eye on the behaviour of the young players. But tennis was so much unknown to the village people that when our aged workman Sam came to put up some netting around the lawn to stop the balls from going through the hedge he asked what it was for; and having had the matter explained to him, he then remarked, 'Ah! I mind now I once yurd a young feller zing a zong about thick, "Way down in Tennessee".'

Country Fairs and Fetes afforded opportunities for young people meeting and enjoying a little fun together. The Fairs were in every case mainly for the purpose of business; but the professional showman made a point of being there, knowing that there would be plenty of people present with money to spend and time on their hands. I delighted in the Fairs and, though my spending money could usually be counted in pence, I always managed to see a good many of the side-shows and to get a great deal of fun out of what was going on. I liked to stand by the tall, tower-like apparatus with a bell at the top and watch the lusty young farm labourers swing the 'bittle' and bring it crashing down upon the peg. The weight would fly halfway up the tower and stop. Several equally strong young fellows would try with no better success. Then along would come a wiry little fellow about half their size. He would watch what was going on for a moment, then step into the ring. Spitting on his hands, he would seize the handle of the great wooden mallet, swing it gracefully and easily round his head and let it fall on the peg. The weight would sail right to the top of the tower and clang against the bell. It was obvious that knack had as much to do with it as anything and that sheer strength was of very little use. The Boxing booths always attracted a crowd of men; I never saw a girl or woman even look at one and certainly not one of that sex would have entered one. One of the regular shows consisted of three men, one of whom was a nigger, and a great bear. I think those who challenged the bear had to wrestle with the animal; but I never saw anyone tackle him. I heard people say that it would hug a man to death if it got its paws round him. I saw one of our men once win a pound for standing up to the nigger. He couldn't knock the nigger out, nor could the nigger floor him; but our man certainly showed more signs of punishment by the time they had finished slogging each other. I think the proprietor gave the man the pound as an encouragement to others to come forward and so as to stop the fight and clear the booth for another lot of customers. One booth was run by a woman and her son, who was one of the boxers and afterwards became world famous.

I generally managed to knock down a cokernut [sic]; but I never attempted throwing at the brightly-coloured 'knock-em-downs' as the rewards were tobacco. I saw the most beautiful girl I have ever seen in charge of a cokernut shy. It was the first time I had ever been really moved by the beauty of a girl and I can still remember her distinctly. Of course, she was a gypsy. Her hair and eyes were almost black and her skin a warm brown that glowed health and seemed to quiver with vitality. Though I was much too young to have ever touched a girl as a girl, I at once felt that to touch that lovely warm, silky skin would be a most exquisite delight. She was standing against the box of wooden balls, one hand resting easily

VILLAGE AMUSEMENTS

"MISSED HIM!"

'Missed him!'

on her hip. I suppose she must have felt me gazing at her; for she turned and looked straight into my face. She wronged me by that look; for I had gazed upon her in perfectly natural admiration for a lovely girl. Her look was scornful, perhaps because I was not of her class and she instinctively disliked me because of that. I blushed furiously and quickly hid myself amongst the crowd; but in that short meeting she had burnt herself into my memory for all time.

Some of the shows had a performing pony; others had two or three performing dogs. In some a man would hurl axes into a board against which stood a bespangled woman; or he would vary the performance by throwing butcher's knives at her, one on either side of her head and one between each of her outstretched fingers. Sometimes the handles of the knives were wrapped with tow and the tow set alight; the woman was then hemmed in by a wall of fire. Then there was the human serpent, or boneless wonder: a little boy who went up and down a ladder, writhing in and out between the rungs and finally sitting on top with his legs folded behind his head. There were two fat girls in pink tights who danced bobit-ty-bob to the tune of a barrel organ in order to attract customers to the 'Wild Beast Show' which consisted of about a dozen small animals and which were all described as being either extremely rare or extremely sav-age. I saw all the little shows in the course of time, though I had to be selective with my patronage as my funds rarely permitted me to visit more than two or three on any one occasion. There was a rigid class distinction attached to swing boats; the young workmen and their 'maids' alone enjoyed them; we were never allowed to go in them.

A COUNTRY CHILDHOOD

Fetes were arranged locally, sometimes as an annual political rally, sometimes in order to raise funds for a local need and sometimes in celebration of some special public event. The professional showmen were rarely allowed to help in these as all the funds were needed for the political party, or the local need, or to provide something to mark the special event. The Fete was one of the real show days for the village band, it had to provide music in the intervals between the pony races and foot events. Perhaps in the evening there would be dancing in the open air to its music and this would be about the only time the village people indulged in this form of amusement. The programme of events was much the same at every Fete: local pony races and flat races for the children, climbing the greasy pole for the men and lads, shooting at a metal pigeon attached by a long cord to a long pole which was made to swing round in a circle and thus provided a rapid flying target at which the young farmers tried their skill. There would be side shows, such as Aunt Sally and Hoop-la. Tilting the Bucket was a favourite competition amongst the men. The bucket, sometimes filled with water, sometimes with sawdust, was balanced on a crossbar, below which hung a short piece of wood with a hole in the middle. The competitor was wheeled under the target in a barrow. He carried a long pole as a lance and endeavoured to thrust this through the hole in the plank; failure to do so meant that he and his wheeler got a soaking or were smothered in sawdust as the bucket tipped over. This was really a very amusing competition, and I have often wondered why it appears to have died out. There was certainly a great deal more in it than in many of the gambling games now so popular at Fairs and Fetes and which seem to have been quite unknown in those days. There were often competitions in needlework and table decorations for the women; very often foot races for the men. A tug-of-war between teams from rival villages, or perhaps between rival trades or occupations, was a common and popular event. Sometimes there was a cart horse parade, which made a bright and interesting spectacle; riding events were also popular. I have seen several good donkey races; donkeys, now almost extinct apparently, were common in the district and some were extremely good trotters. One man fitted a couple of penny-farthing wheels to a little trap and with this light and easy running vehicle easily out-distanced his competitors. At one Fete that was held in a meadow beside a small river I saw a race in tubs propelled by heather besoms; I think most of the competitors fell overboard before the end of the race. I thought I would try that game myself; so I watched for an opportunity after a pig had been killed and took the scalding tub to the

132

shallows at the back of the mill. I pushed off bravely into the stream and within two minutes I went over the side flat on my back into the water. At another Fete, which I believe was to celebrate the jubilee of Queen Victoria, I saw a pets race in which rabbits, cats, dogs, a goat, a goose, a hen, a tortoise, a pig and even a frog competed. The owners had their pets on strings; but this did not prevent a tremendous dog-fight in the middle of the event. I believe the race was eventually won by the hen, which apparently bolted in the right direction when the dogs started to fight. At some of the bigger Fairs there was usually some professional performer engaged to add attraction to the affair. At one I saw a balloon ascend some of the helpers narrowly escaping ascension with it through not letting go their hold on the ropes that were holding it down whilst it was being filled with gas. The balloonist descended by means of a parachute and landed on the other side of the river with no bridge within a couple of miles. At another there was an exhibition of tight-rope walking and the crowd got a great thrill when the performer crossed the rope with his feet in baskets and his eyes blindfolded. I tried many of the tricks I saw at Fairs and Fetes and, of course, had to try tightrope walking. Very soon I could run along the single rail that protected the road from the mill tail, balancing myself by means of the punt pole.

Having reached that stage of proficiency, I discarded the pole and tried walking along the wire rails between the posts that separated the meadows. This was not quite so easy as the wood rail by the mill, as the wires sagged suddenly between the posts as one stepped on them; but I mastered it in the end. Sometimes the Yeomanry put up a show of horse exercises – tent-pegging, cutting off the Turk's head and similar feats. This was always extremely popular; the performers were all well known, they were good horsemen and their brilliant uniform was very becoming. With the exception of those who had the constant care of stock, such as shepherds, dairymen and carters, everybody attended the Fetes. Even an August Bank Holiday Fete, though falling when corn harvest was in full swing, drew large crowds of country people.

Circuses and Menageries, though always located in a town, had certainly a right to be called country amusements; for the country people flocked to them from all round the district. The farmers, with their wives and children, usually attended the afternoon performances. In the evening many of the country working men trudged miles into town after their day's work and back again after the performance. Once, when one of Sanger's great circuses came to the market town, we drove in in the morning so as to be in time to see the midday procession. Mother obtained permission for us to sit in the window of a room over a shop in the main street, so we had an excellent view. This was the first time I had ever seen either an elephant or a camel and I was tremendously thrilled at the sight of these strange beasts. The brilliantly costumed riders on their piebald horses, the clowns, the great gilded cars with perhaps half a dozen pure white horses in pairs or a dozen tiny cream ponies drawing them, filled me with joy. A further excitement was added by a terrific to-do amongst the elephants and camels. I have no clear idea as to exactly what happened; but I can remember that the crowds in the streets became very frightened, the procession was held up for some minutes, the elephants trumpeted, the camels screamed and Mother became very agitated. I think the animals nearly reached the stampede stage. Circuses and everything connected with them became quite a passion with me; so much so that I began to practice many of the acrobatic feats in secret and soon, in addition to my proficiency as a tight-rope walker, I could walk on my hands, turn a standing somersault and ride standing on the back of my pony. I never had any desire to become an engine driver; but I often dreamed of myself as a circus performer. Mother had an absurd adventure with an elephant at the farm. A vine grew up the wall beside the roadway that led past the mill to the river, and the side window of Mother's bedroom looked out through the branches. She was dressing at the time and, hearing the sound of soft rustling footsteps, quite unlike the usual heavy tramp of farm horses, looked out to see what was passing. She was astonished to look straight into the trunk of an elephant stretched up to pluck a branch of vine. The elephants were on their way to the next town and were being taken to the river for a drink. Though I did not happen to see these elephants (I could hardly have been more than two years old at the time), I saw many circus horses taken to drink at the river behind the mill and made friends with many of the circus men. Though I did not always remember them, they always remembered me when they came by for the second time. The Showmen attending the great autumn Sheep Fair came every year and some I got to know so well that, when they saw me later at the Fair, they let me come into their show without payment. My love of circuses was so great that, even if I was unable to go to the performance, I never missed the chance of watching the horses and wagons arrive and seeing the tents go up. Eventually, in a fit of depression following a severe reprimand over some misbehaviour, I decided to leave home and join the circus which had pulled out before daybreak that morning to travel to the next town. I was soon walking fast along the road in the direction it had taken. I had made no provision for food and, when an old woman trying to drive a cow into a field called on me to help, I was glad to do so and accept a few pears for my trouble. I rested beside the road and ate some of my pears before continuing my journey. I had covered half the distance when a thunderstorm came on. I took refuge beneath a tree. It began to get dark and I soon became very miserable, as I have always been extremely frightened of thunderstorms. Presently a horse and van came by and in a particularly brilliant flash that occurred at that moment the driver saw and recognised me. He pulled up and called to me to jump up behind. I was much too miserable and frightened to think of what I was doing and hastily scrambled up over the tailboard and took refuge beneath the tarpaulin. Some time later the driver pulled up again and shouted back to me, 'Here you are. Jump out now.' I jumped out and found myself within a quarter of a mile of my home. Of course there was nothing for it but to go home and face the consequences. I found the whole place in an uproar. My sisters had somehow jumped to the correct conclusion as to what had happened when darkness came on and I could not be found. I heard their howlings before ever I got into the house. 'He's run away from home, I know he has. He gets blamed for everything that happens, poor boy, and now he'll never come back any more'; and the howlings burst out with redoubled vigour. I felt that it was as good a moment as any to make my entrance. It was. I was greeted like the returning prodigal. There was not a word of blame and no questions asked; only rejoicings that I was back safe and sound. Though it seemed a tame ending to what looked like becoming a great adventure, it turned out to have been a very good move on my part; for a considerable time after this event I was remarkably free from reproof and certainly had not to take the blame for the misdeeds of others, as had been so often the case before. I have always thought that Father had a good deal to do with this change of attitude towards me; he had always been extremely careful never to fix blame until he had made quite sure of the culprit. Mother's disposition was more hasty and she was always inclined to jump on the first person at hand when dispensing reproofs. This event took place after the family had left the farm and were living in Mother's house on the outskirts of the market town. Though it cured me of any idea of running away from home, it did not diminish my love of the circus. I still feel that for a long holiday there is nothing I should so much enjoy as to travel round for a season with a circus.

Turtle doves

Chapter XII
The Chalk Pit

T may be safely assumed that the mill took its name from the chalk pit. I have no idea how old the mill was; but a record has been found, dated 1505, referring to the bridge as 'White Mill Bridge,' so I think we are justified in supposing that the mill was already in existence then and the chalk pit already a recognised landmark[11]. If the original face of the pit was in line with the edge of the abrupt slope that formed the high bank in Long Ground, and extended to the main road (that is to say, a distance of about a hundred yards), the depth of the working on the horizontal would be about two hundred yards. But I am inclined to think that the original pit occupied the ground now used as the garden to the two workmen's cottages across the road, and the yard, stables, sties, cowstalls and the lower flower garden belonging to the mill. If this supposition is correct, the pit-face must have at one time extended about three hundred yards. As the working face of the pit has only receded about ten yards over a width of about twenty-five yards in fifty years, I must leave it to others to calculate the length of time that would be required to work an average depth of one hundred yards over a width of three hundred yards. I make it something over a thousand years; but this can scarcely be relied upon, as we have no evidence that the removal of chalk was constant in amount over this period. The present pit is roughly circular in shape; but not more than fifty yards of any part of the diameter was used in my time. The sides had fallen in and formed steep slopes covered with grass and brambles; but the worked face was perpendicular and shining white of such dazzling purity that one soon began to suffer from a kind of snow-blindness after spending a few hours there in bright sunlight. I was very fond of hunting for fossils in the newly worked face and have frequently had to come away

---

11 Evidence from the Domesday Book suggests that Sturminster Marshall had two mills in 1086, one of which was almost certainly at the White Mill site. Many mills pre-date the Norman conquest of 1066.

because I could no longer stand the glare from the clean white chalk. I never found a fossil of any size in the pit; though I always had hopes of coming across the remains of some gigantic prehistoric monster.

I knew that many of these had been found about twenty miles away. I heard of these from others who came there with their hammers and chisels and who always found Father interested in their hobby; but I did not then know that the 'rock' in which these great reptiles were found differed greatly in the history of its formation from the 'rock' of our pit. The commonest fossil was the 'Peter's Finger,' the local name by which the fossilised ink-pot of the cuttle fish was known. These polished, pointed, finger-like objects could always be dug out of the cliff face. I also often found small fragments of thin shell which had obviously formed part of a small bivalve similar to the mussels that could be found in the ditches in the meadows. Once I found a very beautiful shark's tooth, which I gave to the school museum and at once regretted having parted with it. It was rather under an inch in height, was very highly polished, had an extremely sharp point and the cutting edges were finely serrated. Though I often watched the visiting geologists working carefully over every inch of the cliff face, I never heard that any of them made any remarkable finds. My own visits were so frequent that I do not think any fossil of unusual size or exceptional interest could possibly have escaped my notice.

There was a certain element of danger in working in the pit, both to men and horses. I was always very careful to look upwards before approaching the face to make sure that the cliff above was securely anchored. If I noticed a crack or a threatening overhang, I searched for a few large flints or knobs of chalk, and pelted the dangerous spot before approaching; this would dislodge anything insecurely fixed. I saw several accidents of a more or less serious nature. The first made a great impression on me. I was playing in the garden and saw Father go by with a workman and our carter leading our big grey horse. The workman I recognised as one of two I had seen pass earlier with horses and carts towards the pit. I sensed at once that something was amiss and followed them at a discreet distance. When I got to the grass slope overlooking the pit I saw a mouse-coloured horse lying in the stiff chalky mud of the track. Our own horse was standing by and chains were being passed round the horse in the mud. Presently Prince began to pull on the chains and, as the fallen horse was slowly dragged from the mire, I heard it cry out with pain. It was the first time I had ever heard a horse cry in pain and it upset me considerably. A horse is usually silent, even when grievously hurt, and I have only heard the cry twice since. Quite twenty years after this accident I recognised the same horse in the streets of the market town; I had not set eyes on it in the intervening years, but I was not in doubt for a moment. I stopped the man who was leading it and asked him how long be had been working for the owner of the horse.

'All my life,' he replied.

'And how long has he had that horse?' I asked.

'I believe he bred it,' the man answered. 'It was just broken in when I first went to work there and that's more than twenty years ago.'

'Did you ever go hauling chalk from White Mill Chalk Pit with that horse?' I next asked.

'I'd like to have as many sovereigns as loads of chalk I have helped take from White Mill Chalk Pit with that horse,' he said.

'Then perhaps you were with it when it fell down in the pit and they had to get one of the horses from the mill to pull it out.'

'I can remember that very well,' he said. 'I believe that was almost the first job that horse did. Father was there with me and he went across to the farm and they brought along a big grey horse to pull ours out of the mud.'

'The big grey was one of my Father's horses and I was the little boy in the sailor suit who stood on the grass slope and cried.'

The man was very much surprised and interested and told me that the horse was about twenty-five years old and still able to do a good day's work on light jobs.

On another occasion a man came running in from the pit wringing his hands and crying, 'My God! My God! My mate! My mate!' Father asked him what was the matter; but could only get a repetition of the hand-wringing and exclamations. I was very busy making up some fishing tackle at the moment. Father turned to me and, telling me to run to the stable and get men, picks and shovels, went off to the pit with the distressed man. When I arrived there a few minutes later with one of our men and some tools, I saw the fellow's mate almost buried in a great heap of chalk. The face of the cliff had given way and in falling it had cut off the tail of the dung cart they were loading 'as short as a carrot' and buried the man with the exception of his head and one hand. Blood flowed freely from a cut in the man's forehead, and he was groaning as if in great pain. Father, our man and myself set to work at once digging him out; but the poor fellow's mate was too upset to do anything but pace about and continue with his hand-wringing and exclamations. I have never seen anyone so completely demoralised at the sight of an accident. When we had liberated the prisoner, he was taken to the house, where his wounds were dressed and he was given something to revive him. After resting for an hour or so, he was able to go home in one of the carts and, with the exception of some bruising and shock, was little the worse for his adventure.

Chalk for use on the estate[12] of which the pit formed a part could be obtained free of charge; but when taken elsewhere a charge of a shilling a horse-load was made: that is to say, if a single horse was used one shilling would be charged and if two horses, two shillings. One-horse loads were not common, as even the ordinary two-wheeled dung 'pot' required two horses to drag it out of the pit if the track was muddy. I think that a shilling was sometimes saved by sending two carts and three horses. The third horse would help in drawing both carts from the pit and the strongest horse would pull one cart once it had reached the hard road. One of the rules was that the first thing to do was to see that the cliff face was kept perpendicular. This was a safety precaution and meant that the first job was to climb up into the field above the pit and knock away the top edge. But this was often too much trouble and the common practice was to back the cart under the cliff, stand up in it and hack away at the face, and hope that the resulting downfall would not be so great as to do any damage. It was neglect to remove the top edge that resulted in the accident to the man who was buried.

At the entrance to the pit there was a level plot of grass, which no doubt formed the bed of the pit some hundreds of years ago. As the pit faced almost due South it was always a warm spot and this grass plot was used as a nursery for our young chickens and ducks. The coops, with little slatted runs in front (I don't think galvanised wire was known in those days; as chicken runs, rabbit hutches and similar articles were all made with wood slats), were set out on the grass and each day moved, so that the ground beneath was always fresh and sweet. I used to like to go with old Sam when he went to feed the chickens. Sam carried a bucket of mash in one hand and a bucket of clean water in the other, and always a little straight stick of hazel about a yard long. The hazel stick was really of very little use when chickens had to be fed. With pigs it was different, and it then came in very useful to whack an opening in the pressing, squealing mass through which to pour the food into the trough. But Sam never went anywhere about the farm without his little stick and, as if to make an excuse for its presence, he would sometimes rap the top of the coop with

12 The Kingston Lacy Estate, now owned by the National Trust.

THE CHALK PIT

Moorhens feeding

it, saying, 'Come on there' to the hen inside before he threw in the mash and poured fresh water into the little earthenware saucer. The hens never required any calling to breakfast; as soon as the sack which covered the front of the coop had been turned back, they would begin popping their heads first out of one opening between the slats and then out of another, as if hoping that they would get at the food quicker through one opening than through another.

Further in towards the modern worked face of the pit there was a large circular depression in which grew a tall willow tree. The edges of this depression were hung over with brambles, and except in the very middle of summer, it formed a shallow pond. Moorhens often sheltered beneath the brambles and swam out on the pond. Sometimes a water rail could be seen there. Had the pond been permanent, I am sure I should have stocked it with small fish; but in dry weather the water disappeared and the mud at the bottom cracked into a curious pattern of almost regular squares.

People visiting the pit for the first time always noticed the heap of large cut blocks of stone lying there and enquired their origin. They had originally formed part of the rolling bay which held up the water and drove it down the millstream and under the water wheels. During a big flood the bay broke and, as the landlord refused to go to the expense of reconstructing it, the mill, as a water mill, ceased to exist. This accident may have occurred in my lifetime[13]; but I certainly never saw the water flowing under the mill, except in times of flood. I believe the term 'rolling bay' is unusual; at any rate I have never heard it used except in reference to our own dam[14]. There were weirs attached to all the mills along the river: but they were always referred to as 'weirs.' There was one very striking piece of evidence of the force generated by floods. For some years there lay,

13 Not quite: Keith Eldred's research suggests it occurred in 1865.

14 The term 'rolling bay' is also used to describe a similar feature at Fiddlefard Mill, about twenty miles upstream.

wrapped around the upstream point of the big island, a gigantic chain. The metal composing the links of this chain was possibly half an inch in diameter and the length of the chain itself may have been fifty feet. It is easy to imagine the great weight of this amount of metal. It had originally been placed across the river more than half a mile further upstream to prevent cattle straying down the shallows on to other people's property; yet a flood had swept this mighty weight down the river until it had been stopped by the point of the island. No doubt it was carried away by an uprooted tree and this helped to transport it downstream.

There were several other chalk pits in the neighbourhood, most of them situated up towards the downs; but our pit was very much the largest and most frequently used. The reason for this was that our pit was nearest to the acid, peaty ground in the heath country beyond the hills on the other side of the river. Chalk was particularly good as a dressing to the fields in this sour district and often in winter for weeks on end there would never be a working day in which there were no carts loading chalk from the pit. When the weather was wet, this constant traffic turned the cart track through the pit into a dreadful morass of white mud of the most amazing tenacity. I often tried to cross the muddy ruts of the track by running lightly over them as quickly as possible; but in most cases I either missed my footing or did not travel fast enough, with the result that I would have the greatest difficulty in dragging my feet on to the firm ground. Then even the toughest and most luxuriant tussocks of grass failed to clear off from my boots the evidence of my prank and I knew I was in for a scolding when I came indoors.

There were bunches of moor rushes growing near where the rolling bay stones were piled and in these a hare sometimes sat. One might have thought that a hare would have been too nervous to sit in the close vicinity of so much active work; but hares place a great reliance in their invisibility when crouched in their forms and I have frequently found them sitting in places quite near to where people are constantly passing. Provided a hare is not disturbed it will return again and again to a favourite seat. Later I was to find that our chalk pit was not peculiar in providing attractive sitting-places for hares: I have frequently seen them sitting in the rough grass in chalk pits in Kent.

In early summer sparrows nested in numbers in the cracks in the face of the cliff; the presence of their nests being nearly always betrayed by a careless straw protruding from the entrance. The thick growth of brambles and wild roses that clothed the old workings made ideal nesting places for numerous thrushes, blackbirds and warblers. There was also almost every year a turtle-dove's nest there. In winter, when food was scarce, the droppings made by the horses and the grains of corn scattered from their nosebags attracted the rooks and jackdaws. One might have thought that the jackdaws would have nests in the cracks in the chalk as the sparrows did; but the jackdaws of that district appeared to be tree nesters and any tree that had a suitable hollow in it would almost certainly be appropriated by a pair of these birds.

The country around my home was somewhat noted for the Stone Age relics which were found there from time to time. Quite a number of people took an interest in these. The famous Flintstone Jack, whose forged specimens of early stone implements are, I believe, still to be seen in Salisbury Museum, frequently travelled that way with his counterfeits, which in some remarkable manner always happened to be just the very thing that someone wanted to complete a particular series. Though I do not remember having seen him myself, Father apparently knew him quite well; he also spoke of another man who travelled the roads with a double octave composed entirely of flints and on which he played tunes by rapping them with a little hammer. From time to time the ploughmen brought in flint arrow heads turned up in the course of their work. I once found a perfect specimen of a double-edged flint axe. I did not know it as such when first I picked it up. I noticed that it had been shaped; but did not know that this shaping had any particular significance. What attracted me chiefly was the lovely note it gave out when struck. I kept this stone for several years in a thorn bush in the chalk pit; taking it out, when I thought of it, and carrying it about with me so that I could strike it and hear it ring. Later on I saw its double amongst a collection of early stone implements in a museum. I then decided that it was worth looking after; but, when I went to my thorn bush, it had disappeared.

'The baker's cart'

Chapter XIII
The Bakehouse

HERE was no place quite so welcome on a cold day as the bakehouse; it was always warm and cosy in there. Local people often stopped during a shower to take refuge in the stables, which opened right on to the main road; but, if it was really cold weather, many of those who could claim any sort of acquaintance with Father, turned off the road and went into the bakehouse to enjoy the warmth and have a chat before continuing their journey.

The bakehouse was a low, square building with a window looking straight out on to the river. Sometimes Father shot a snipe from the window as it was feeding on the muddy shore of the little island exactly opposite; he excused a sitting shot by saying that he could never hit one flying. He was very proud of me when I brought in the first snipe I shot flying. The oven stood nearly opposite the door of the bakehouse. A stout iron door closed its mouth and inside was a deep and low cavern paved with flat stones. It was heated chiefly with faggots of furze cut on the downs and kept in stacks on the spare ground between the mill and the river. The next best fuel to gorse was thorn, plenty of which could be obtained when the big hedges in the meadow were being cut. Most of this fuel could be bought very cheaply, as it was useless for general household purposes; a nominal charge to cover the cost of putting it into faggots was all that was demanded. When the faggots had burnt themselves out, the door of the oven was opened and any embers that remained were raked out by means of a long-handled iron tool, curved at the end into a half circle. These embers were thrown into a recess at floor level below and slightly to one side of the oven. Sufficient heat remained in them to stew things slowly, and frequently an iron pot filled with small potatoes stood over them. The cooked potatoes were used as food for the pigs and poultry. A second implement was used to clear out the small embers still remaining in the oven and to cool the floor slightly. This consisted of a long pole to which was attached a short length of chain and a piece of sacking. The sacking was dipped in water and then pushed and turned about over the floor of the oven until every glowing cinder had been 'douted' and swept out. The oven was now ready to receive the batch of loaves.

The dough had been made and put to rise first thing in the morning. On three sides of the bakehouse were long wooden bins raised on short legs from the floor. One of these contained cake tins and other sundries, another contained flour, and the third was used as a receptacle for the dough whilst it was rising. When removed from the bin, the dough was placed on the lid of the next bin and kneaded by an action of the wrist that closely resembled the movements of a cat's feet as it works them when comfortably seated on one's knee: we always spoke of our cats as 'kneading' when they did this. As the kneading proceeded, lumps of dough were torn off and flung upon the scales, and it was surprising how frequently an experienced man could remove exactly the amount to make a loaf. This lump was again torn apart, the largest portion remaining under the left hand. After further kneading, the smaller right hand portion was put on top of the larger left hand lump and a final dig given with the knuckles to produce the depression always found in the centre of the top of a cottage loaf. Loaves were made in two sizes and, when I first knew anything about the bakehouse, only cottage loaves were produced there; loaves baked in tins came into fashion considerably later.

The loaves were introduced into the oven by means of long-handled wooden spades known as peels, and were removed by the same means. The peels and rakes, when not in use, rested on an iron framework suspended from the roof of the bakehouse.

Cakes went into the oven after the bread had been removed; they required a gradually declining heat. The square or oblong cakes were baked in separate tins; but most of the round cakes were baked in round hoops of tin placed on a long iron tray. Before the tins were ready to receive the cakes they had to be greased and for this purpose a spare tin was kept filled with lard and a piece of cloth ready in it. This tin was placed in the oven for a few minutes, in order to melt the lard, and then every tin and hoop was quickly wiped round inside with the cloth. Large sheets of paper were placed on the iron trays and a strip of paper was placed around the inside of each tin hoop. To line the hoops with paper the baker first cut the strips to the right size and then, twisting them with a quick movement around his left hand, dropped them into place. The whole operation was completed in about two minutes. The standard cake was the plain 'dough' cake; but twice a week a rather more elaborate selection was produced – madeiras,

Young Robin

plain buns and a few more tasty varieties. From time to time there was an order for a Christmas or wedding cake. A very popular cake was made by remixing any unsold cakes, adding more currants, and spreading this mixture between two thin layers of paste on one of the large iron trays. When this had been based, it was cut into squares, which sold freely at a penny each. These cake squares were rather more 'puddeny' in consistency than ordinary cakes; but were very good eating. A couple of these and a hunk of bread and cheese made a grand lunch on a day's rabbiting or fishing. Our own pies were often baked in the bakehouse oven; but I never remember seeing a joint of any kind cooked in it and was rather surprised, when I went to live in Somerset, to find that it was a common practice in the villages to have joints cooked at the local bakehouse. When the bread had been taken from the oven and placed on the tops of the bins to cool, the small bags of flour had to be weighed and put ready for loading up into the carts. I enjoyed helping with this. I was never trusted to do the weighing; but I was allowed to close and stack the bags. The closing of the bags was done by picking them up by the two corners of the mouth, swinging them round twice to fold over the edges and then, with the first finger and thumb of the left hand pressing in the corners of the mouth, the right hand ironed out the bag until it became the shape of a broad, flattened brick. The bags were then piled up in rows at the back of the bin, the self-raising flour in one lot and the plain flour in another.

147

When all was ready for the loading I was again made use of. The cart would be drawn up outside the door and one man would take his place in it. Another man, or myself, stood in the doorway and the third stood by the bins. The beginner started by throwing one loaf at a time. As soon as he became accurate he would be promoted to two. The two loaves had to be thrown so that they remained touching each other throughout their flight from the hands of the man at the bin, into the hands of the man in the doorway, and from his hands into those of the man loading the cart. It did not take long to learn this trick; but the really skilful loader could throw four loaves that would travel as one throughout their course. I eventually became sufficiently practiced to master this trick. Meanwhile all these loaves, cakes and bags of flour had been entered in a book, and perhaps a bag of meal, ordered by some pig or poultry keeper, had been brought from the mill and placed in the cart. Then the horse was brought round and harnessed in and the man was ready to start on his journey. Two carts left the bakehouse every morning, one crossing the bridge to travel the round of the villages, farms and cottages on that side of the river, and the other making a round of the district on the mill side. The hour of their return varied from about half past four to perhaps half past six, according to the delays they met with on the road.

Father was really the Master Baker in the bakehouse, though he employed two qualified men; but he had always taken a great interest in the work himself and, though primarily brought up as a farmer, had become more proficient as a baker than either of his two employees to whom baking was a whole-time job. He was not content with making just the bread and standard cakes demanded by his customers; but frequently tried his hand at some new kind of cake, bun or tart. His pastry and cakes were always excellent and Mother, though she had every reason to be proud of her own cooking, always admitted that Father had the better 'cake hand.' Father modestly explained this as being the result of his possessing the type of hand essential for the production of good work: cool, supple and neither dry nor moist. All his cakes were mixed with his own hands, which he kept in good order by washing them in the barley meal and skim milk in the pigs' barrel. This barrel rested on an iron frame on two wheels and always stood outside the mill ready to be filled with the fresh meal. As he passed the barrel, Father would dip his hands into the clean, sloppy mixture and vigorously rub them, and he would dry them by continuing the rubbing until all the moisture had been evaporated or absorbed by the skin. I doubt if any creams could produce such a good result as did this simple process.

House martins and swallows

Though white bread was the rule, because nearly everyone asked for it, Father was no believer in it. 'We take out the germ and nourishment of the wheat and feed it to the pigs,' he would say, 'and keep the rubbish for ourselves. Who would ever think of trying to fatten a pig on white flour?'

I never learnt any baking; my jobs in the bakehouse were always of a very simple nature. One I liked very much was removing the round cakes from their tin hoops on the long trays. In nearly every case a little of the cake had oozed out between the hoop and the tray and this I was allowed to eat. It was very sweet and crisp and formed a nice snack at about eleven o'clock in the morning, which was about the time the men knocked off for a few minutes' rest and a mouthful of bread and cheese.

One day I threw something into the hot embers in the recess below the oven door. A cloud of fine dust sprang up and some of it got into my eyes. Father told me I was silly to have done it and then, pointing to some black specks under the skin on one temple, said, 'Do you see that? When I was about your age I took my father's powder flask and tipped some of the contents on to the embers in this place. There was an explosion and I lost all the hair of my eyebrows and was blinded for about six weeks. They thought at first that I should never see again. Those black specks are some of the gunpowder.' Father frequently added a tale such as this against himself after lightly rebuking me for some foolishness. He never made himself out to be superior to anyone, not even to children; which perhaps explains why he succeeded with everyone, including children. With very small children he had odd little tricks which always seemed to amuse them. One of these was to snip at the child's nose with the knuckles of two fingers and then show the child his thumb-tip in the same place, saying, 'I've got your nose.' The child would invariably put up its hand to its face to make sure its nose was still there and then its face would break into a smile when it realised that this was only play. With young boys he was wonderful and all my schoolfellows adored him. He could get down to their level and joke with them and yet always manage to keep them in order and happily employed. My special school friends were always given a day's perch fishing in the summer and a day's ratting in the winter, and both these little treats were looked forward to eagerly because Father always came with us and helped us with the boat or the tackle, or looked after the ferrets.

On Good Friday everyone, rich and poor alike, had to have their hot-cross-buns. This meant that the bakehouse staff had to work all through the Thursday night. As soon as the men had returned from their rounds and had had a meal, they set to work preparing the dough for the Friday's batch of bread. When the bread had been taken out of the oven, the buns went in and, as the small buns had to occupy the same floor space as the larger loaves, it was necessary to bake several batches throughout the night. Father worked with the men and the baking was usually finished and the loaded carts started on their journeys by eight o'clock on the Friday morning. The crosses on the buns were made when they were in their uncooked state by stamping them with an instrument something like the date stamps used in Post Offices for cancelling stamps though the bun-stamp was five or six times as large as the date-stamp. During these long nights the men often became very sleepy and on one occasion it was noticed that the man crossing the buns seemed to be spending an unusually long time at one part of the batch. Father went over and discovered him sound asleep, but still stamping away energetically though without moving from the same spot. He had chopped the bun in front of him into two small pieces. But, though they had had to work twenty-four hours without any sleep, the bakers had finished their rounds on the Friday by midday, and so could then have the whole of the afternoon for rest. Our hot-cross-buns never failed to appear on the breakfast table on Good Friday morning.

I very often helped the bakers harness their horses to the loaded carts; for sometimes the carts were loaded before the horses were 'hatched in,' as they used to call it. On one occasion it happened that the cart was very heavily loaded in the tail with a sack of meal and other things. The horse was brought round and I was told to hold up the shafts. With a great struggle I managed to do this; but I had not raised them high enough for the horse to pass under them. 'Hold them up higher, boy,' said Father. I did so and felt myself leaving the ground. In a flash I saw myself catapulted through the air an unknown distance and perhaps finishing up with a broken neck - it is really amazing how quickly an active-minded child can think in an emergency! I let go. The tail of the cart crashed to the ground and out flew the loaves, cakes and bags of flour. Some landed in the water of the mill tail. It was the only occasion I ever heard Father use a swear-word and almost the only time I ever saw him lose his temper. 'Damn the silly fool of a boy!' he said; 'Get along out of it!' I bolted round the mill and made myself scarce for the rest of the day. Father said no more about it; he never dragged things up a second time and he probably realised he had asked too much of me. After all, I was only about nine years old at the time and a heavily-laden, two-wheeled cart can tax the strength of a man when he gets the full weight on his hands.

'Feeding the pigs'

Chapter XIV

Work

ORK on a farm never ceases. Whatever the weather, whatever the time of year, there is always something that needs doing. The art seems to lie in never letting things get into such a state that some job is never done, or left so late in the particular season that to do it then would be useless. As our farm contained within it a mill and as the work in the mill could be carried on without reference to the state of the weather, it was often the custom to switch over some of the farm hands on a wet day to attend to the grinding in the mill. Two men were usually sufficient for this job; one to work downstairs, feeding the engine and filling the sacks with the fresh meal as it came out hot from between the stones. The other man fed the stones from above and took charge of the filled sacks as they came up through a trapdoor in the floor. Except for those men who had to face the weather to attend to the stock, the other men were employed as much as possible under cover, dressing corn in the barn or doing repairs to harness and such-like in the stable. Father would never keep a man out in the wet if he could possibly avoid it.

Ploughing, harrowing, sowing and rolling went on, according to the nature of the crop, throughout the whole of the autumn, winter and early spring. Wheat was always sown as soon as the land could be got ready in autumn; there was a local saying that young wheat should be high enough in March to hide a sitting hare. This, of course, referred to a hare that was feeding and not to one crouched in its form. A hare in its form is almost invisible on practically bare ground. Hares move about and feed a good deal by day during March; so it was not difficult to test this saying on a field of young wheat. Mangolds also had to be hauled early and safely clamped before the frosts came. In the winter the sheep would be folded on the swedes and these had to be pulled and heaped in readiness to be put through the turnip-cutter. The pulling of turnips was an art that required some practice before one could become really useful at it. The root was pulled from the ground by the left hand and the root-tip trimmed off with a stroke from a short 'hook' or chopper. The root was then swung against the blade of the chopper in such a way that the green top remained in the hand of the puller and the clean root sailed through the air and landed exactly on the heap some yards away. Whilst the sheep were still on the swedes, the lambs would begin to arrive. If the flock consisted of horned Dorsets as was often the case, most of the lambing would be over by Christmas; but with the hornless Hampshires, lambing would start usually just at the end, or beginning, of the year. To go and see the sheep was a daily job with every farmer in the district. The fertility of the soil largely depended on this animal and it was rightly looked upon as of very great importance. On those farms which kept really large flocks of sheep there was often a complaint by the men who were in charge of other live stock that the shepherd always had first pick of everything and they had to put up with his leavances. This was often very near the truth: if the dairyman and shepherd both happened to run out of hay at the same time, you may be quite sure that the shepherd would get his without delay and the dairyman when a man and a horse could be spared for the job. Fortunately this state of affairs never arose with us. Our flock rarely exceeded seventy-five ewes and it was not difficult to look sufficiently far ahead to provide for the wants of these without having to upset some other job in order to furnish them with supplies. In our case also the dairy farm was quite separate and almost self-contained so far as food supplies were concerned. Only one, or at most two, milking cows were kept at the mill farm, to provide milk for our own use and for the baker and carter who lived in the two cottages across the road.

A rather curious coincidence occurred one year in connection with farm work. Just at the beginning of the corn harvest I went with Father to the next farm in order to watch a new invention in operation. It was a self-binder and was the first to come into the district. In some cases the self-binder was resented by the workmen. Already gleaning had almost died out. When I was quite small the labourers' wives came with all their children to clean the fallen ears of corn, from the grain of which they helped to keep the almost universal pig and often a few poultry. When sheaves were hand-tied a strong young woman could often earn a few shillings to help out her husband's weekly wage. Though good, or at any rate comparatively good, wages were earned at harvest, anything extra was always welcomed; for it was the harvest money that provided the family with winter clothes and boots. However, the self-binder had come to stay and as soon as the early difficulties had been overcome, which seemed to con-

'Peewits spiralling down'

sist chiefly in the continual breaking of the twine, they began to appear on every farm. That same autumn I went with Father to a farm a good many miles away across the downs and there saw a team of oxen ploughing. 'Take a good look at that, my boy,' said Father; 'You may never see it again.' It was not a team worked as a sort of fad by a moneyed man; but a regular part of that farmer's economy. Father, of course, remembered working oxen as a regular feature of almost every farm in his young days and my Mother's uncle had been quite famous locally as a breeder of draught oxen. For years I had a portrait of one of his oxen which I greatly treasured and should do still, had it not disappeared, as so many old family things do, at the breaking up of our home. This picture was done in pencil and water colours by a travelling artist and, although it was a picture of what the proud owner believed his beast looked like, rather than what it really looked like, it was a very delicate piece of work. The ox, with lovely little curls all over its flanks and a back as flat as a table, stood in front of the farm on which it had been bred and which appeared as a careful pencil drawing showing between the legs of the coloured animal. These travelling artists made a living by going from farm to farm painting the portraits of favourite, or champion, animals. In some cases the surroundings were painted at the artist's home during the winter and he travelled the country adding the animals to them during the summer; the surroundings in these cases would be creations of the imagination and not actual scenes, as was the case with the portrait I had.

With the dairy farm situated over two miles away, I saw very little of that part of the farm work. I was rarely there, except when we were harvesting in the fields attached to it, and then was too busy 'leading and driving' to have time to look round the dairy or watch the milking. The term 'leading and driving' referred to the work of leading the loaded wagons from the field to the stack-yard and driving the empty wagons back to the field to be filled; it also referred to leading the wagon between the aisles of stocks in the field whilst it was being loaded. The hardest part of the job was when one had to make a sharp turn out of the field gate into the road with a loaded wagon. This required a good deal of management, as the horses were inclined either to turn too sharply or else to carry on too near to the opposite hedge. In either case there was considerable danger of turning the load over, which might easily have resulted in serious damage to horse or wagon, perhaps both. Some of the horses were very easy to manage and would steady up at once when spoken to in a quiet tone; but others required very firm handling. Old 'Flat Foot' was my terror. He was a very strong and hard-working horse with feet so large and heavy that he seemed to have no control over them. He could never be made to draw a load steadily; but would pull with all his might, snorting and flinging out his great feet in all directions. I had to struggle with all my strength when getting him through an awkward gateway, one hand holding his bridle and the other pushing against the shaft of the wagon. I always managed to avoid upsetting the load; but I carried away several gate posts and often found myself swung off my feet by this energetic monster.

I got to know all the cows at the dairy, because they were always brought to the mill farm each year during their dry periods; so that, although we had only one or two milking cows in the meadows at home, there were nearly always half a dozen of one kind and another there. The dairy herd consisted mainly of shorthorns and all that we bred ourselves were by a shorthorn bull of the favourite roan colour; but there were always a few cows that showed traces of breeds other than the shorthorn. One big-boned, black and white cow might well have been a cross-bred Friesian; though I do not believe that this breed had been introduced into the country at that time. For some years we had a Hereford, a pretty beast with a white head and a white streak along its back: but Herefords were beef cattle and not much thought of as part of a dairy herd. A couple of black Kerries were in the herd for a few years; but Father had to get rid of them because they were so much inclined to break out and this induced the other cows to do the same. 'Brindle' was a cow that always interested me. She was quite different from any other cow I had ever seen and I often wondered what breed she was supposed to represent. She was yellow in colour and speckled all over with little black lines; she was a big cow and had very long and thin horns pointing almost straight forward. Had she been savage, she would have been a terrible creature to encounter; but she never seemed to know what fearful weapons she carried on her head. Another cow with very long horns was a strawberry roan; but her horns swung out wide on either side of her head and gave her a very wild look. She also was very quiet and seemed to find her great spreading weapons rather a trouble to her, as they were always bumping into door posts and gate posts.

The main stock of pigs was kept at the dairy farm. Sometimes the herd numbered a hundred in all. When the young pigs were ready for fattening, they were brought up to the mill in batches of ten. Being all the same size, they had less difficulty in competing for their share of food: their progress also could be watched more easily. With meal almost hot from the mill stones and a plentiful supply of warm cooked food they put on weight at a great pace. After the harvest had been gathered in the pigs were sent out on to the stubble in charge of a boy. One of these boys found that an old sow made a comfortable and quiet mount. He would spend nearly the whole day on her back and, when he saw that some of the smaller pigs had crept through a hole in the hedge, he would whip up his steed and ride round them to turn them back. Another boy suffered from fits. One day he was sent on an errand over which he seemed to take a very long time. Someone went to look for him and seeing the pigs very busy in a group in one part of the yard, drew near and discovered the boy unconscious beneath them. The pigs had torn off most of his clothes and would no doubt soon have started eating him; for pigs will not hesitate to eat flesh if they can get it. The poor boy was little the worse for his adventure, but, of course, it was not safe to keep him on.

Hedging and ditching were two jobs which went together and called for a good deal of skill. Chorl was our champion hedger and ditcher and often proved his abilities at local competitions. To make a satisfactory hedge it is necessary to have an eye for the future growth of the hedge after the old wood has been cut out. The hedger first looks the hedge over and makes up his mind what will have to come out and what should be left. He then cuts out and pulls back all the old and unnecessary growth, leaving a number of well-grown thorns, ashes and hazels standing. From what he has cut out he now selects strong forked sticks and cuts a number of hooked pegs. The standing sticks, from which the new hedge is to be formed, are now cut part-way through and bent down, when they are pegged into place by the hooked sticks. This layering or 'plashing' must not be done haphazard; the hedge is required to keep stock from breaking into growing crops and it is therefore necessary that the plashing should be so laid and fixed so that it will be impossible for an animal to climb the bank and step over it. Chorl's plashings always stood out at about half a right angle from the crest of the bank; so that, should a bullock step on to the side of the bank, its progress would be barred by the projecting plash-ings catching it just above the knee and preventing it from raising its leg. When the hedge had been properly plashed, the ditch was cleaned out so as to form a true drainage for the water and the turfs and sods so placed on the bank that they would stay where they were placed. Chorl left no tempting tufts of grass sticking up from a sod inviting a bullock to pull at them and so bring out the side of the bank with a shower of loose earth; neither did he throw his sods up anyhow on to the top of the bank where they would dry out and come rolling down as loose earth, or heat and rot the sticks of the growing branches he had so carefully pegged into place.

Chorl was also the thatcher for the farm and he was very good at this work; but he did not go in for the flourishes to be seen on the ricks on the farm next to the dairy farm. These ricks were really something to admire and wonder at. They were all built upon staddle stones and so beautifully rounded and shaped that they looked as if they had been cast in gigantic pudding basins. The edges of the thatch were perfectly even and the top-most point was crowned by a little twisted spire or sheaf. But Chorl's thatching, though lacking in this neat finish, was perfectly weather tight and safe against any winds, and that was the purpose for which it was intended. In addition to the harvests of hay and corn, we had also harvests of withies and rushes, which were harvested every year. The withies had to be cut carefully so as not to injure the trees, a sharp upward cut close to the main stem being the correct method. The young shoots were cut from the willows and bound into bundles. The trees then looked like knobbed stakes driven into the ground. Next year a fresh and more plen-tiful crop of shoots would be produced from these stakes. There was no basket-making industry in the immediate neighbourhood and the bundles of withies were all sent away to factories in another part of the country. The rushes were sold to a local man who came when they were ripe, cut them, tied them into sheaves and stood them in stooks along the banks of the river to dry. The rushes were used for making baskets and the seats of chairs. Every workman carried a rush basket on his back and nearly all the chairs in the cottage had rush seats. These rush-seated chairs were very much more comfortable to sit upon than those with hard wood seats.

There was usually a certain amount of piece work available on the farm, so that an industrious man could add to his wages doing some of this as overtime work. Hedging and ditching, hoeing and pulling straw for thatching were the chief piece work jobs. A man was often given the choice of doing a job at a day wage or as piece work. Casual labour, except at haymaking, corn harvest and threshing, was usually paid at piece work rates. Father employed very little casual labour, nor was it the custom in the district to do so; but there was one man who always came to us for haymaking, harvest and threshing. This man led a curious life. He had no home; but could usually be found through the man who owned and hired out the threshing machine, as he generally kept in touch with the latter, so as to lend a hand when wanted, or when he felt like it. He worked only in fine weather and during the warmest part of the year; only during a really prolonged period of rainy weather would you be likely to see him about, when he might be driven to work through lack of means to provide himself with food.' He always spent the winter in the Workhouse. He was a good workman and very strong. I do not remember ever hearing him speak and I don't think he ever did, unless someone spoke to him. He was not disliked by the regular men, but none of them attempted to make friends with him nor even to carry on a conversation with him. I believe this is a kind of snobbery; he was really a sort of working tramp and the regular workmen did not associate with either tramps or gypsies.

The workhouse also cast a stigma upon anyone entering, and a person connected with the regular labouring class would suffer anything rather than go into one. This man eventually died in the Workhouse, which the workmen seemed to think a crowning disgrace: but which was probably a much more comfortable way of dying than in a ditch, which might well have happened in his case. His place as our extra hand was taken by a youth who had been running errands for the village shop. This fellow had tremendous strength, but was quite devoid of intelligence. People in the towns always regarded the farm labourer as a dull-witted fellow and considerably lower in intelligence than the town workman, and shops requiring a boy always advertised for a 'smart lad.' This attitude is not yet quite dead. No doubt village shops also required 'smart lads' and this fellow may have been smart enough to deliver groceries; but he certainly was not smart enough to do the work required of him on a farm - he made a mess of everything he tried to do. I think Father had a good deal more patience than most people and I know that he never sacked anyone unless he was absolutely obliged to do so; but this lad was too much for him. He stayed with us throughout the haymaking, harvesting and hoeing. In farmwork you learn more by watching how a job is done rather than actual instruction. The average farm labourer does not waste many words on a pupil: he takes the tool and, by using it himself, shows how it should be used; then he passes it on and expects a pretty good showing even if it is only a first attempt. This is a good way to learn; but it necessitates keen observation and close attention to details on the part of the learner. It was obvious that this fellow had very poor powers of observation. If there was the slightest possibility of doing a thing the wrong way, you might be sure that he would stumble on that way. When the carter was told to take this fellow along to help with a job, I heard him remark, 'A poorish tool 'e be - strong in the arm but thick in the 'ead.' That summed him up pretty well. He was not re-engaged the following year; one of Chorl's boys was old enough to go to work and Father was glad to have him and so have a reasonable excuse for not calling on the other.

When the land was too wet or too frozen in winter to be worked, the yards were cleaned out and the manure carted to the fields and there dumped in small heaps ready for spreading. Dung-hauling was one of the hardest jobs in farming. The sodden, trampled-on muck was surprisingly heavy to lift and was so matted together that a good deal of effort was often required to separate a forkful from the mass. Though the smell was unpleasant, no one objected to that; it was what was to be expected. To a townsman there are many scents about a farm that are unpleasant; the choking smell of animals in a stable, the bitter smell of folded sheep, the cow-stalls and pigsties, and the musty smell where fowls habitually roost. But these everyday smells, though objectionable in themselves, through associations become almost pleasant to the farmer and farm-workers. I have always a distinct sense of pleasure when I smell one of these scents, though the scent itself may be objectionable. About the only obnoxious farm scent that is really obnoxious to the farmer is the scent of fusty hay. This is a scent indicating something is amiss and here again I suppose it is an association of ideas that makes it objectionable; hay ought not to go fusty and, if it does, someone is to blame for carelessness in the making or slackness in opening the rick in such a way as to let the weather in. Our hayricks were always opened on the North or North-east sides, where the cut would be protected from the rain-bearing storms from the South and South-west.

Threshing was an autumn or winter job, according to the nature of the corn to be threshed and the time when the machine would be available. The 'drausher,' as the machine was called, was kept by a farmer as an additional source of income to that derived from his small heathland farm. I sometimes went with Father when he drove to this farm to make arrangements for hiring the threshing machine. It was always an adventure, because the country was quite different from our own. Our fields and meadows gave one a feeling of long-settled farming and quiet fruitfulness; but this place looked rough, wild and untamed. There were big woods all round and many of the fields were rough and poor-looking. Though the farm was distant only about three miles from our own, it seemed quite cut off from regular contact with the rest of the world. The soil was dark and sour-looking; whereas ours was very light in colour by reason of the closeness of the underlying chalk to the surface. Badgers and roe-deer inhabited the deep woods and Father always asked if any had been seen lately. To

'Badgers... inhabited the deep woods'

me these animals seemed to be real wild beasts, creatures of the wilderness and exciting to hear about. Once we were given a haunch of venison from a roe that the farmer had shot a day or two before. The little deer had been in the habit of coming to drink at the farm pond. The farmer had seen its footprints and had lain in wait in a nearby shed. The children at this farm were wild and shy. They did not speak to us; but stood there silent and staring. Visitors to the place were unusual and the children gaped at us as no doubt I should have gaped at one of their badgers or roe-deer. When I went to school, these little trips with Father could take place only in the holidays and some years passed without an opportunity of going again to the farm; but it seems that I had not been forgotten. One evening Father started smiling and chuckling; we knew that he had a little joke inside that would come out in good time. 'I didn't know you went in for sweethearts,' he said to me. Then he took out his handkerchief and began to untie a knot in the corner, from which he extracted a half-sucked sweet. 'Here is something a young lady gave to me to give to you,' he said as he handed it over. 'I've been over to Bartlett's this afternoon and the children stood under the hedge and stared as they always do. Just as I was leaving, one of the girls put her fingers into her mouth, pulled out the sweet she was sucking and, handing it to me, said, "Please Mister, give that to your boy." Then she went as red as a beetroot and bolted. There's love for you!' I had certainly never given her any encouragement; for I was much too shy myself to speak to any girl, unless she spoke first, and even then I found considerable difficulty in carrying on any sort of conversation.

WORK

On the day fixed for the threshing everyone had to make an early start. A good supply of sacks had to be looked out and taken to the rickyard; the stable boy got out the water can and, backing it into the river at the drinking place, stood on the shafts and filled it with a bucket; the long ladder was taken out from the shed behind the stables and, having been set up against the rick, one of the men mounted it and commenced strapping the thatch. Meanwhile the engine and threshing machine were got into place. As soon as the water arrived, the fire was lit and everyone waited for the first signs of steam, which indicated that work was about to commence. I have always considered the rising and failing hum of a threshing machine one of the most musical of all agricultural sounds. In fact, I think it is about the only sound of farming that can claim to be musical. The swish of milk into a pail is very pleasing, so is the regular harsh hiss of a scythe passing through moving grass. The clanking of a roller, the quick throb of a winnowing machine, the chug-chug of a turnip cutter and the rattle of a mowing or reaping machine were agreeable sounds, but none of them approaches the musical quality of the hum of the thresher. My interest in the threshing did not come to life fully until the rick was nearly finished. I might have a few odd jobs to do as the work proceeded; but everyone knew that as soon as the rats began to move my whole interest would be centred on them. Killing rats has always been a passion with me for as long as I can remember. A country boy is brought up to regard the rat as one of man's worst enemies and to kill it whenever possible. He learns also to kill other creatures; but with most of these he is taught to study restraint. Rabbits and hares he will spare when they are young, or when they are not particularly required as food. The sight of a rabbit or a hare does not immediately produce a desire to kill. Even if the rabbits are seen to be doing damage to a young crop and their destruction is necessary, the arrangements are made calmly and without heat as a normal farming job. But the mere sight of a rat is enough to stir up an overwhelming desire to slay it and every possible available means is at once employed to bring about the creature's end. An occasional rat would break away from the stack as the work of threshing proceeded; but the main body clung to the shelter of sheaves until the faggots that formed the rick-bed had been almost reacted. Then the slaughter began. A terrific commotion took place as each rat appeared. If a dog was present he was 'lieu-lieued' from several directions at once as several rats broke away simultaneously from different points. A short, thickish stick was the best weapon and a sweeping action a more sure method of hitting the rat than a downward stroke.

I was not very particular as to how I killed a rat, provided it was killed. If in the excitement of the moment I slung my stick from my grasp, I was quite prepared to grab the rat with my hand. I knew I was perfectly safe if I brought my hand down over the rat's head or shoulders and kept the animal down. I would pull a rat out of a hole by the tail; but I knew it was not safe to pick one up by the tail in the open. I have fallen on a rat and kept it under me until a dog could be brought to kill it. I have had a rat under my right hand and another grabbed with my left as I lay sprawled upon the ground and then had to raise myself carefully until I could set one knee upon one of the captives whilst I dealt with the other. I now look back upon my daring in this particular direction with considerable surprise, because I cannot understand how it came about that though I seemed to be afraid of most things that most people are afraid of and of quite a number of things that most people are not afraid of, I had very little fear of an animal that seemed to really scare most people.

My practical knowledge of farm work never reached a very high pitch. School from the age of nine kept me busy in other directions most of the time and it was only during the holidays that I had any chance of taking a hand with what was going on. I think it had been arranged for a long time that I should not become a farmer, and so I was not encouraged to take any practical interest in the work of the farm and only called upon to help when it was necessary, as at harvest time, to rope in every possible man and to get the work done quickly. I learnt a few of the practical jobs of the farm by lending a hand during school holidays. Chorl taught me hedging and this I thoroughly enjoyed. It was so satisfying to see the ragged hedge cleaned up and gradually taking shape again as a sound fence. Chorl had no use for careless work. He was a prizewinner himself at this work and wouldn't have a hedge that he had a hand in making looking anything but a compliment to his skill. He constantly cast an eye over my section to see that the plashings were level on top and in line with the bank, and he went over the stakes again with his own 'bittle' in order to 'firm' them properly.

A regular job for me was minding the engine on grinding days. Though I cannot remember that I ever aspired to be an engine driver, this job always kept me happy because it was not too exacting. The engine did not require constant attention; provided the water tubs were fairly full and the steam gauge kept steady to its mark, there was not much else to do. In between stoking and refilling the tub, I baked potatoes in the hot embers that came through the boiler pipes and settled in the front part of the engine. I also usually had a rod set on the bank of the hatch pool within sight from the engine and this required attention when the disappearance of the float or violent bobbing of the top indicated that a fish had taken the bait. If I happened to be trying for perch, I could usually provide myself with minnows as bait from one of the engine tubs. The water for these tubs was dipped up in a bucket from the river. In order that one could dip at once into fairly deep water, a plank had been set upon short posts and jutted out into the river. Utensils from the bakehouse were also washed from this little jetty and many minnows collected there for the scraps of dough washed out. These minnows, growing careless by reason of the food often following the introduction of a bucket into the river, frequently found their way into the buckets that were used to fetch water for the engine.

When apples had to be gathered, I could always make myself useful either in the trees handing down the fruit, on the ground packing the baskets, or in the punt conveying the cargoes to land. I wonder in how many places in England they carry their apple harvest home by water. At winnowing I liked either to turn the handle of the machine, or to scoop up the grain with the broad wooden shovel and tip it into the polished wooden measures. I was not strong enough at that time either to move a filled sack, or even to tip the measured bushel into the sack. I learnt to pull and trim swedes, and here again Chorl was my teacher. I was pleased when I could land nine out of ten of my trimmed swedes right on to the heap. When Chorl was ill one spring, I took over the flock of seventy-five ewes and their lambs for about a fortnight. I learnt then that every sheep is different and by the time this duty was ended I think I could have placed the right lambs with the right mothers in about half the flock. I also learnt hoeing but can't say I liked the job. Stooping all day with a hot sun on one's back is uncomfortable and however much energy you may have it is useless hammering away at this job. The hoe must be used with sufficient vigour to uproot the weeds and surplus roots, but not to throw them haphazard over the neighbouring rows of roots; and great care must be exercised dislodging a weed growing closely alongside a root that has to be left growing in order not to damage or displace this root.

Timber felling and hauling were done by trained men and horses and were a most interesting operation to watch. Whether the tree had to be felled, or was one already fallen which had to be trimmed, the skilful work with axe and saw was a revelation as to what a saving of energy can be effected by long practice. The axes swung and fell with effortless ease, and chips almost as large as fire logs flew off as if they had been no harder to cut than a turnip. The long cross-cut saws sang as they sank deeply into the wood, the men seeming merely to swing backwards and forwards without any muscular effort. But the horses were more wonderful still. One of the men told me that it took anything up to six years to train a horse to a stage when it could be trusted to work with its head and take the responsible position in the team; the quickest learners required about three years. These leading horses seemed to be able to understand everything said to them. There is considerable danger both to men and horses in raising heavy timber on to the carriages; a too-eager or inattentive horse may pull the great log too far, or twist it sideways. These timber horses were rather on the small size, stocky and quick on their feet. It was a most interesting experience to see the leading horse throwing its weight into the chains, pulling steadily as directed, holding the great tree motionless at a signal and slacking the chains directly the call came that the load was safely in place on the carriage. In some of the work a great wire cable was used. Once, whilst standing by watching the felling of a tree, I put my hand on the tight cable. A shout from one of the men made me remove it quickly. Had the cable moved suddenly through my hand, the sharp projecting spikes of broken strands, nearly always present in a cable that has been much used, would have ripped the skin from my palm. We had a little cart horse called 'Stumpy' which Father said would have made a splendid horse for timber work. Father bred it himself and it was a great favourite with all the men because of its willing and quiet disposition. It was transferred from general farm work to take our milk twice a day to the factory. Though it had spent all the earlier years of its life working at a steady walking pace with farm implements, it retained an ability to trot well and made a very good horse for the lighter, though rather quicker, work in a milk cart.

I never learnt either to milk or plough; in fact, about the only horse-drawn farm implement (carts and wagons not included) that I ever operated was a horse-rake. This is not altogether a simple job for a small boy, as the reach of the handle and distance of the footrest from the seat are built to accommodate a man. Several times I pitched out backwards through losing my balance on the slippery iron seat whilst working the heavy lever that raised the teeth to allow the rakings to fall in line with that already swept up. It was that wild old devil Flat-foot that caused these slight mishaps; it was quite as much as I could do to manage him without having to attend to the rake as well. After this I was always allowed to have 'Stink-foot.' She was a quiet old creature and never gave the slightest trouble in any cart or machine. Her real name was Violet; but she suffered from a dreadful swelling, smelling sore on one of her feet, which sometimes caused her a good deal of irritation and which had to be dressed periodically with a poultice of fresh cow-dung. I learnt to groom a horse and liked grooming the cart horses and pony; but I hated having to go near one of the bread-cart horses because he always tried to bite. The men said that it was because he was a bit ticklish; I considered it was just bad temper. I could harness a horse into any sort of cart or implement, adjusting the straps in the base of a two-wheeled cart so that the balance of the load rested on the axle and not on the shoulders of the horse.

The feeding of pigs and poultry was a pleasant and light task. I think the pleasantness of it lay in the obvious pleasure of the creatures being fed and the eager way in which they gathered about one's feet. At other times the domestic birds and animals did not always appreciate too close an approach by a human being, even though they might never have received rough treatment. Young bullocks, which will frequently bunch and bolt when being driven from one place to another, will crowd around the same man when he enters their field with a forkful of hay on his back. It is astonishing what an enormous bundle of hay a skilled man can collect on a pitchfork and carry on his back; he appears to be almost buried under the mass as he walks down the road. Even old Sam, though all the time I knew him he was always too old for work, could put together and carry a load far heavier than he could raise from the ground. He would fill his fork, then stand around fiddling with odd jobs till he heard somebody coming up the road. He would then get the other party to help him raise the great bundle on to his shoulders and totter away quite comfortably, with the greater part of the upper half of him almost hidden from sight. I have heard clever people giving details of the amount of fresh meat and beer it is necessary for a man to have in order to do heavy manual work; yet these farm labourers of years ago rarely touched fresh butcher's meat and drank very little beer. Their favourite drink in the field was cold tea or a temperance drink known as 'botanic.' Most of them were extremely strong, most of them worked till they were seventy or more, and most of them, excepting that four out of five had rheumatism in their later years, were very healthy.

'Cunning versus strength'

Chapter XV
Village Industries

suppose that one time our village[15] was much the same as any other village of any size and contained within its boundaries examples of almost every kind of ordinary trade and occupation. Before the coming of the railways the villages and surrounding country to a great extent had to be self-supporting so far as the everyday requirements of life were concerned. I do not remember times quite so primitive, but for all that one could buy most ordinary articles in our village and what one couldn't buy ready-made one could nearly always have made by some handy man or woman. The countryman has always seemed to have a greater capacity for picking up the knack of doing things than the townsman, perhaps because to do the thing oneself is so often the only way out of a difficulty. Even to-day you will rarely find the countryman quite stumped by the breakdown of a piece of machinery.

I think there was only one craftsman in the village who gave his whole time to one job. The wheelwright was also the carpenter, builder and undertaker. The grocer sold also ironmongery, boots, ready-made clothes and harness; he was also a 'colley-maker,' or repairer of harness; he also repaired boots. But the man who gave his whole time to one trade was one of the two blacksmiths, and this was because he had a sufficiently large trade to enable him to do so. He even employed an assistant. The other blacksmith filled in his time with odd jobs; lending a hand with the hay-making and harvest, etc. The full-time blacksmith's shop was always a busy scene and everyone who passed the door of the forge stopped to look in for a moment and watch the sparks gushing up from the fire. The assistant worked the bellows and attended to the fire, damping it down with fine wet coals after each horse had been shod. When a shoe had to be made, the smith took a long bar of iron from a corner, thrust one end of it into the glowing coals and, having brought it to a red heat, removed it

---

15 Sturminster Marshall.

with a pair of tongs and held it over the anvil whilst he cut off the required length. After repeated heatings the piece of iron was beaten into the required shape; but before it was tested on the horse's hoof, it was plunged into a trough of water to be partly cooled. The heat still remaining in the metal was, however, sufficient to burn the horn of the hoof. The smell of burning horn was rank and offensive until one became used to it. As the smith applied the shoe to the hoof and examined the fit, he had to blow vigorously to clear off the clouds of smoke that billowed up into his face. At last a perfect fit was obtained. Then the shoe was again heated and holes punched to take the long square-headed nails. The punch was a hard iron tooth and was held by a handle formed of a hazel stick twisted around it in a groove made for the purpose. The shoe was then held in place, the nails driven in, the points turned down and afterwards smoothed off with a heavy rasp. I was always fascinated by the operation; but could hardly believe that it was not painful to the horse. Most horses, however, stood quietly whilst they were being shod and, though their ears were usually laid back and they certainly did not appear to be enjoying the operation, they gave no other indication that it was painful. One part of the process always was, and still remains, a mystery to me. When the smith was hammering a red hot shoe he allowed his hammer to 'run down' on the anvil. The effect was that the shoe would be smitten perhaps twice and the anvil would receive a connected series of little blows before the shoe was again attacked. The carpenter did not do this when he drove in a nail and the only reason I could find for the smith doing it was that he liked the noise. Nothing in the nature of ironwork came amiss to the blacksmith and there were always a few ploughs, harrows and other imple-ments standing outside the forge waiting to be repaired. If an iron brack-et was required to support a shelf in the dairy one did not go to the iron-monger and purchase a cheap japanned article. One went to the black-smith and gave him the exact measurements and he would then produce a bracket complete with a spike for driving into the wall, holes to take the nails or screws, and sufficiently strong to stand the weight of a man. The blacksmith made me a grand eel spear with five prongs each with a set of finely cut and tempered teeth to hold the eels.

The 'Colley-maker's' shop was a wonderful place. Shelves ran right up to the ceiling and the contents were divided into departments containing in one groceries, in another medicines, in a third nails, screws and tools. From the ceiling hung hams, bacon, baskets, boots, pots and pans, buckets, ket-tles and various small tools, rakes, prongs, forks, picks and spades stood in one corner; salt fish and boxes of bloaters were stacked in another. Balls of twine and string hung from a hook in the doorway. Cheeses stood at the end of the counter. In the window were cottons, threads, needles, buttons, scissors, knives, boot-laces, dubbin, blacking, harness soap, cheap linen underwear, straps, braces, belts, bridles, halters and crockery. His work-shop was detached from the shop; but looked out towards the road so that he could see anyone entering the shop. His place was known as The Shop, because it was the only real shop in the village. You could buy sweets, paper, ink and a few other small items at the Post Office; but that was The Post Office and was not considered as a real shop. The oft-heard remark, 'I 'low you'd get un up shop,' was true in the majority of cases.

The wheelwright was an artist at his trade. His strong line was wagons and they were really magnificent, with superb curves and perfect finish. They were brilliantly coloured in blue, red and yellow with the maker's and owner's names clearly lettered and decorated with many graceful scrolls. I have never seen any wagons anywhere to equal those made by our village wheelwright. They were as well balanced and beautiful as ships, and as ships they always appeared to me as they were drawn majes-tic and heavily laden across the fields or along the roads. The timber used was all selected according to the particular part of the wagon it was required to make and the finished article was so strong that it could be depended upon to outlive its owner; in fact, quite a number of the wag-ons in use in the district had been handed on from father to son. Besides wagons the wheelwright also made carts, wheelbarrows, gates, doors and coffins. He made our punt, a broad, flat-bottomed affair that it was almost impossible to upset and with a lidded box at one end with holes in the bot-tom to allow of a constant supply of fresh water so that fish could be kept alive in it; the closed lid being used as a seat. The wheelwright also did every kind of carpentry repair work, indoors and out. In those days there was no nonsense about a job being outside the scope allowed by a Trade Union: if a man could do a job he did it and most village craftsman could handle any ordinary tool with considerable skill.

There was a butcher in the village; but his trade was chiefly in old cat-tle that could not be offered to a farmer's regular butcher customer in the town, or in animals that had met with some accident or had been chilled and had to be slaughtered to save the carcase. He could sell his goods only to some of the village people; the farmers bought their fresh meat on mar-ket days and usually had a joint from one of their own animals, if possi-ble, from the butcher to whom they regularly sold. If one of their own sheep or bullocks was not on sale, the butcher would name the farm from which a particular animal had been bought; the farmers liked to know on whose farm their joint had been produced. Their purchases would be sent round to the hotel at which they stabled their horse and placed in their gig.

There was one Public House in the village and another, which called itself an hotel, opposite the railway station; but the railway station was never looked upon as a part of the village as it lay at the extreme end of the houses and was not known even officially by the name of the village.[16] The Public House[17] stood exactly opposite the church gate and did a reasonable trade with the villagers in beer and tobacco. Sometimes a shooting or fishing party would call for a bread and cheese lunch. They were always given a little room at the back. No respectable person outside the working class ever entered the bar; it was one of those things that was not done. 'Going into pubs' was not the thing that a man would do who valued the respect of his neighbours. And he did not sneak in by the back way so that none might see him. If he wanted a drink he sat on his horse or remained in his gig and the drink was brought out to him: so that any passer could see what he had and how much of it. The 'hotel'[18] by the railway station was chiefly used for the purpose of stabling the horses of those who drove in to catch a train. It was a much more modern building than the old Red Lion and had no doubt been built shortly after the railway had opened.

There was a second 'colley-maker' in the village. He had only a workshop; but he was a good workman and made a reasonable living from it and various odd jobs. The remaining 'industries' of the place were carried out by individuals who had perhaps other regular work, but who were known to be able to do certain things or provide certain goods. There would be a woman who could do simple dressmaking; another who made and sold a herbal ointment; a man who kept a few hives of bees and from whom honey could be obtained; another who made a special side line of his garden and who had always a supply of plants and seedlings in their season. One old man could repair rush-bottomed chairs and another had a good reputation as a saw setter. In some village, there is a regular export of articles made in the cottages, but I do not think that anything was made in our village beyond what was required by people living in the immediate neighbourhood.

---

16 The station was known as Bailey Gate.

17 The Red Lion, which is still a pub today.

18 The Churchill Arms, sometimes known in the past as The Railway Hotel.

VILLAGE INDUSTRIES

Spotted flycatcher

The main industry of the place was of course, agriculture. There were perhaps about sixty or seventy houses and cottages and of these about ten were occupied by the craftsmen and others already mentioned. Two were dairy houses, the herds together being about sixty cows. Apart from the schoolmaster, the constable and a few retired people and old ladies, all the other members of the community were directly connected with the land and every morning the three roads that led out of the village from the central green, on which stood the Maypole, were traversed by little parties of labourers setting out to their work on the farms in the vicinity. The parson lived outside the village, the vicarage being situated beyond the railway station and about a mile from the church. The village might have been described as comfortably industrious. No one appeared to be particularly anxious to make money quickly: to obtain enough to live on and to enjoy life seemed to be the general principle. No one seemed to be in a particular hurry and two friends meeting could always spare the time to stop and chat for a few minutes: but, so far as I know, there was only one really lazy man in the place and he was the illegitimate halfwit who for his own and others safety was eventually placed in the care of the county Asylum. I have always felt that this comfortable industriousness is the most sensible way of living. A few women were lazy. 'Chorl's' wife was one of them; she could always find time to stand in the road with arms folded across her sack-like figure and look at - well, I've never made up my mind what she could have looked at, as there was only an occasional pass-

173

er-by to see and I am sure she was not the sort to take an interest in the birds and trees. But most of the women attended seriously to their homes and kept them and their children clean and tidy. Village children, though often clad in the cast-offs of the more well-to-do members of the community, or the cut-down and made-up remnants of their elders' garments, were always cleaner in person and clothes than the majority of town children of the working classes. Villagers, on the whole, had a great deal more self-respect and independence than the same class of townspeople.

There was a milk factory right against the Station yard; but this, as with the Station itself, though both employed men from the village, never seemed to form part of the village itself. These too-modern forms of activity did not fit in with the quietness and old-time air of the village itself. Though both might claim to be country institutions, they had no connection with antiquity and smelt too much of the industry of towns. There was an air of money-making about them; whereas true country work has always conveyed to me the impression that it is a method of obtaining a living and that the money side of it has relatively little importance. This was well illustrated in Father's and many other good farmers' attitude towards the use of artificial fertilisers, at that time attracting considerable attention. He and they admitted that these artificials increased productivity; but they 'punished the land.' At all costs the land must be kept in good heart; it had nourished men for countless generations and it was their duty to see that it would continue to do so. Now that we have had time to see effects of the general use of artificials, the danger of robbing the land of its 'heart' is being more fully recognised. Dung and lime were two essentials. As Father said when discussing the merits and dangers of the too-free use of artificials, 'A man may think he feels all the better for a glass of whiskey and he may be at times; but you have only got to look around to see the results of its continual use.' The more modern and specialised type of farm conveys this same idea of money-making rather than just a wholesome means of making a living.

There used to be a dentist in the village; but I never saw him operate and think that he had gone out of business before my time. He lived in one of the row of cottages just opposite church and was, I believe, a carpenter by trade. The operation of tooth-drawing was simple and primitive. The patient sat on the top step of the dentist's cottage; the operator then took the poor fellow's head between his knees, seized one of the tools from his bag and ripped out the tooth as he would have pulled a nail from a plank. Meanwhile anyone passing by stopped to watch the proceedings. I imagine that an attack of toothache must have become quite unbearable before the victim summoned up sufficient courage to face this public ordeal. An aching hollow tooth was often eased by being filled with a plug of black tobacco, which no doubt deadened the nerves.

There was no resident doctor; the doctors came from the nearest towns and their carriages were well known on the country roads. Any medicine ordered was fetched by the poor, half-witted woman whose son was the village lunatic. She, almost daily, pushed her dilapidated pram into town and brought back such medicines as had been prescribed. On her way home she would collect sticks from the hedges for her fire. Her living must have been a poor one and she often begged assistance from Father, which I think was never refused. I have many times seen him hand her a loaf, or a quarter-pound of butter, a rabbit, or half a dozen eggs. If others treated her as well as he did, she was certainly never in real want of food. On one occasion news was brought to Father that the son had been seen with a new loaf and a roll of butter, which Father had that day given to his mother, melting the butter on the still warm bread and scooping out the resulting pap with a spoon. His mother, poor creature, could do nothing with him and often bore evidence of his rough handling. It must have been a relief to her when he was put away; though I remember that she cried bitterly when she told Father that they had taken her poor Joe and 'putt 'en in to 'sylum.'

There was a local hurdle-maker; but I did not recognise him as a native of our village. I used to see him sometimes in the wood making his wattle hurdles, bay cribs and thatching spars. It seemed an ideal occupation on a warm, sunny day to sit thus in the quiet of the woods and weave the rough hazel sticks into such interesting and useful forms. His method was to buy the standing coppice wood and make his goods on the spot. News that he was at work in a certain wood would soon get round and the farmers would go there and make their purchases from the stacks piled up where the living wood had lately stood, or give orders for any special articles required. Later on a wagon would be sent to bring home the purchases or completed orders.

'Willows were plentiful beside the river.'

Chapter XVI

Trees

OST definite districts have distinct types of trees. In one area you may find that conifers predominate; a little further on you come to a district in which beeches are the commonest trees: the next may contain chiefly oaks. No doubt it is all a question of soil and, as you pass from one type of soil to another, so the type of trees will have been found to have changed. I have heard it said that large elms indicate a deep and rich soil. The broad valley through which our river ran must have been exceptionally blessed in this respect, for one of its main features was the splendid elms that grew in the field hedges and beside the roads. Some people who look upon roads as merely tracks for use in getting swiftly from one part of the country to another, say that there ought not to be any trees bordering them. I hope trees will never be abolished from our roadside hedges. A fallen tree may sometimes block a road and wet fallen leaves can be a danger to fast traffic; but the one can be removed in a very short time and a little more care in driving and not quite so much tearing hurry removes the danger from wet leaves. Set against this the delight that the traveller gets from the beautiful views so often to be seen between the trunks of trees along a road, the beauty of the trees themselves, and the comfort of their shade to the pedestrian on a hot day; even the speeding motorist draws up for his mid-day snack beneath the shade of a welcome tree. One of the grandest of all the elms in the district was the one that grew from the centre of the plot of land between the mill and the river and on the top of which the starlings congregated every evening throughout the winter. Father remembered when he could put his arms and legs round this tree and swarm up it. When I knew it the trunk was so massive that I doubt if three men could have touched hands round it. Its roots had extended to the river bank on one side and to the bank of the mill-tail on the other; so that for three parts of a wide circle around it, it was surrounded by a tall fence of its offspring. To one of these young trees that grew from the river bank the punt was chained.

This tree grew at a right angle for about a foot from its base and this short horizontal piece formed a very convenient step and the perpendicular main stem a comfortable support to grasp when getting into or out of the boat. The great branches of the parent tree spread out to meet the branches of the surrounding shoots, so that a deeply shaded space was formed almost around its trunk. There was another row of very fine elms standing a few yards back from the river nearly the whole of the way down the narrow meadow below the bridge known as Lower Ground. A single large elm stood nearly in the middle of the furthest little meadow known as Higher Ground. There were also a great many fine elms all along the valley road which made delightful pictures of the many half-timbered and thatched cottages and added greatly to the effect of the views of the meadows and river.

By a curious coincidence both the mill and the dairy house had Lombardy poplars growing near them, two just alongside the bridge by the mill and four between the buildings and the road at the dairy house. So far as I can remember there were no other specimens of these trees anywhere else within several miles. I noticed that almost invariably artists sketching the mill from just below the bridge shifted the poplars to the other side of the road. I did not understand then that in order to make a picture it is sometimes necessary to give a twist to a road, alter the position of a gate, or remove or change the position of a tree. The Lombardy poplars could scarcely have been called beautiful; but there was a certain grace in their tall, slim uprightness. Sparrows always nested in them and filled the narrow spaces between the almost upright branches and the main stem with their untidy bundles of straw and feathers.

Willows were plentiful beside the river. Some were allowed to grow naturally and formed large and graceful trees thickly clothed in summer with small, narrow leaves on long and supple branches. A good many had been pollarded at a height of about ten feet from the ground and from their clubbed tops threw out a great number of upright branches which were cut every few years to form posts and rails for fencing. The willows for basket work were grown by planting stakes about three or four feet long and cutting off the shoots every year. Many of these annual growths would be six or eight feet long and the best 'rods' would be those having no side shoots. The little island, the marshy spots on the big island and the mill-tail had all been converted into withybeds. The mill-tail had silted up since the Rolling Bay broke down and its conversion into a withybed was a very satisfactory way of making use of the resulting boggy space.

Alders were to be found chiefly beside the meadow ditches; but were not by any means common. They rarely grew much higher than about thirty feet. Ash trees were not very common either. There were a few stumps along the high bank in Long Ground and the growths from these were cut from time to time to provide fencing poles. An ash tree grew in one of the hedges of Seven Acres and, when the field had been sown to oats or wheat and the crop was ripe, I always built my hide for pigeons somewhere within range of this tree. Pigeons, before dropping down into a field to feed, will always pitch in an ash tree if one is available. They like the ash because the foliage is so open that they are able to see around them and so can inspect the neighbourhood for possible enemies before starting their meal. There were also one or two large hollies along the same hedge and from these we usually obtained our supply of berried twigs for Christmas decorations.

The steep slopes in the garden were well furnished with trees, the most beautiful of all being the limes. In the early summer, when the lime trees came into flower, all the bees in the neighbourhood congregated there and the air was filled all day with their musical humming. The limes grew a great thicket of shoots from their bases and another thicket grew from where the first main branches left the trunk. These shoots and the broad, light green leaves formed such a dense shade that it was quite impossible to see up into the tree. Often a pigeon could be heard cooing somewhere in the middle of this leafy shelter; but the bird could not be seen, even if one happened to be up in the tree at the time.

Two yews formed an arch over the gate to the gardens of the workmen's cottages across the road. They were quite large trees and were undoubtedly of considerable age; but the yew in the village churchyard was much larger and probably much more ancient. Nearly every village churchyard had its yew tree and I was told that they were planted in the churchyards in the times when our ancestors used bows and arrows, so that a supply of yew wood could be relied upon when required to make new bows. Occasionally a yew could be seen growing in a cottage garden and there were some apparently growing wild in some of the covers towards the downs. Though the country people always spoke of the ewes in a flock of sheep as 'yows,' they referred to the tree as a 'yew.'

A good many oaks grew beside the valley road. Their acorns were collected by the village children and sold to the farmers as pig food. Care had to be taken when feeding pigs on acorns; only a few handfuls at a time mixed with their other food. Pheasants always found the fallen acorns and, as one drove along the road, they could be seen slipping through the hedge

Blackbirds mobbing a brown owl

out of sight, there to crouch in the rough herbage until the supposed danger had passed. There was a wood beyond the downs consisting almost entirely of very ancient oaks, many of which were hollow. Rabbits often entered these hollow trees and a ferret put in at the foot frequently bolted a rabbit from the branches, the rabbit sometimes running along a thick branch before leaping down. It was considered good shooting to kill one of these 'flying rabbits.' They were, in fact, very difficult to hit; for they presented a most unusual shooting problem as they descended almost vertically to the ground.

Beech trees were not met with till one got well on to the higher ground. The upper turnpike road had a long avenue of beeches. These trees looked very lovely when the first frosts had tinted their leaves. Elms often turn yellow at one particular spot when the early frosts catch them. When the leaves fell from the trees in the avenue the wind blew them into deep drifts in the drainage clutters beside the road. We liked to wade along these drifts of crisp, dry leaves, kicking them before us and making a puffing noise to imitate a train.

TREES

The dark mass of many firs could be seen in the distance from the mill; they formed a dense wood on top of the hill that formed our horizon in that direction. A tall tower stood up above the firs and was one of our weather indicators; when it looked very clear and near rain would almost certainly follow within twenty-four hours. But the nearest firs were in a small plantation on the way to the downs. These firs must have been planted during my lifetime; for, when I first knew them, I could walk amongst them and see over the tops of all but the tallest. In later years I was to stand beneath their lowest branches and shoot rabbits as they ran between the trunks. A few fully grown firs stood in the mixed clump in the centre of the 'camp' on the downs. It was in one of these that the ravens always nested and in another was built the only heron's nest I ever saw in the district. Of lesser trees there were a great many. Perhaps the most interesting were the hawthorns. There are few scents to equal that of a 'May' tree in full bloom on a warm night in early summer. Very few of the hawthorns were allowed to reach the stature of trees in the field hedges; but in the meadows there were many growing on old and twisted trunks that must have stood untouched for many generations. The hawthorn is one of the longest-lived of all our trees. A clipped hawthorn hedge made a neat, compact and impenetrable fence and was often used for this purpose around gardens. In winter the ripe haws attracted many birds. Occasionally a tree would sport pink flowers. Blackthorns also were common. I have found that many people confuse these two trees, or rather the names of them. The blackthorn is the 'sloe' tree and, unlike the hawthorn, it produces its flowers before it shows any signs of leaves. Good walking sticks were cut from the blackthorns and the sloes were gathered, after they had been touched by a frost, in order to make sloe gin. Though we sometimes ate a few of the sloes we did not enjoy them; they left the mouth dry and sent a curious shiver down one as the teeth sank into them. Afterwards the sight of a sloe would produce the same shiver and sense of dryness about the mouth.

My favourite small trees were spindle wood and wayfaring tree. The gypsies cut the straight stems of the former to make meat skewers. The berries were the most lovely of all bush berries. Outside they were a rich pink colour and inside there was a rich orange coloured cluster of seeds. The wayfaring tree first produced an attractive flat cluster of creamy flowers which later developed into a bunch of bright red and shiny black berries. The guelder rose was another small tree that produced red berries as bright as those of the red currant, but of a rather deeper tint.

A really important small tree was the elder. It was useful in a great many ways. The hollow stems (made hollow by pushing out the soft pith) could be fashioned into quite a number of toys including a passable whistle pipe; though I never succeeded in making one on which it was possible to produce anything resembling a musical scale. The leafy boughs were used to repel flies and gnats and the berries for making elderberry wine. Mixed with apple juice they were also used for making elderberry jelly, or with the apples themselves for making jam. They were said to be good for the blood if swallowed whole, but dangerous if crushed by the teeth. The flowers were used by the village women in the preparation of a cream for the cure of chilblains. The flowers (without stalks) were placed in unsalted lard which was melted and kept in that state for a day at the side of the stove. Dog-roses trailed over every hedge and their flowers varied from the palest and most delicate pink to an almost deep red. I never heard of any use being made of the berries, or hips; but the hedge mice found them very useful in winter. It was a common thing to find an old thrush's nest filled with the broken shells of rose hips; mice having carried them there so that they could break them open and eat the seeds in seclusion and safety. Sallows, or pussy willows, were not by any means common. A few could be found, chiefly in sour boggy places in the meadows, and these were hunted out just before Palm Sunday so that the so called 'palms' could be used as house decorations. Though sycamores, or tree-maples, were not by any means common in our district, almost every hedge held bushes of the little field-maple the leaves of which turned to lemon, orange, crimson and purple in autumn. Sprays of these beautifully coloured leaves were often picked to go with a branch of spindle berries as house decorations. Some cork-barked elm bushes growing in a hedge beside the road leading to the downs always attracted my curiosity on account of the strange ridged growth of the bark. The various calls made by insects on the branches and leaves of trees and bushes also excited my interest. The leaves of willows often had little bright red blisters on them; oak trees had oak-apples, marble galls, little tufted, or scaled, galls somewhat resembling fir cones, flat spangle galls, and round bright red galls very much like red currants. Dog-rose bushes usually had a few mossy bedeguars which were picked and carried home. Bramble sprays had curious swellings covered with small holes on their stems. In many of the hedges there grew sweet briars. One of the grassy lanes a short distance from the farm was called Sweet Briar Drove on account of the great quantity of bushes that grew along its banks; we always made a journey there every year to smell the fragrance that filled the air. There were hazel bushes in almost every hedge; but the roadside bushes rarely provided nuts ripe enough to keep, they were picked by the children as soon as the kernels had formed and whilst they still contained their milky juice. There were a few crab apple trees in the covers that had been allowed to grow naturally and which produced fruit which was often gathered to make crab apple jelly; but, though they occurred sometimes in the hedges, most of these were trimmed down when the hedge was being 'made' and so rarely reached the fruit-bearing stage. Though many years later I learned to appreciate the beauty of the wild cherry, which grew in such profusion in the woods of Kent and Surrey I do not remember it as a tree of my home neighbourhood. There was a solitary white poplar that grew on the next farm and was always known to us as the 'rain tree,' because we were told that when the wind turned the leaves so as to show their silver undersides it was a sure sign of rain. As this tree grew nearly a mile away from home, the sight of these white leaves nearly always prompted the exclamation, 'Look at the rain tree! It's going to rain. We had better go home quickly.' Gorse grew plentifully on the downs and in some places to such a height that we could walk about between the stems with the flowers and prickles well over our heads. The smaller gorse bushes were often so closely nibbled by the sheep that they looked like trimmed garden shrubs. Perhaps by reason of having to travel well over a mile to see a gorse bush in flower, this lovely sight impressed me from my earliest years; I suppose everyone admits that it is one of the most beautiful sights of our countryside. When the flowers had finished their purpose and the bushes were covered with dry seed pods, I used to like to walk amongst them and listen to the popping to be heard on every side on a hot summer's day as the pods split and scattered their contents far and wide. In early summer there were always linnet's nests in plenty in the gorse bushes, their proximity often being indicated by the sight of the pink-breasted cock bird sitting and singing from the highest spray of one of the bushes.

Though I like to walk over open moors and rolling downs, or across the bare salt marshes and level sands by the sea, I prefer to be in the neighbourhood of trees, and the larger the trees the better I like them. Even a garden without good trees, no matter how beautiful the flowers, has very little attraction for me. Unless compelled to do so, I would not live in any district that was not well supplied with trees.

Spring flowers

184

Chapter XVII

Flowers

believe that I am right in saying that a chalk or limestone soil produces a greater variety of wild flowers than any other. At any rate our district was very well provided both as regards varieties and numbers. We were particularly well off because we had water flowers as well as land flowers. I expect there were a great many interesting and perhaps rare plants to be found about the fields and hedges; but children do not seem to observe these things very closely and we only looked for and saw such flowers as were used for house decorations or had some peculiarity that attracted our attention. Some flowers were pointed out to us as 'poisonous'; others because they could be eaten. The chief poisonous ones were Lords-and-Ladies, the wild arums that grew in every hedge, first sending their greenish sheaths containing curious fleshy spikes and later showing a cluster of brilliantly red berries. We carefully picked off the sheaths from the flowers and carried about the purple spikes with their rings of hairs and seeds at the base; but the ripe seeds we avoided. Snakes were supposed to be the only creatures that could eat these seeds and they were therefore called 'Snakes' food.' Another poisonous berry was that of the purple iris. This also was red, though of a more orange tint than that of the Arum. The seed head was in the form of three lobes which each split open and showed the double row of seeds lying alongside. 'Deadly Nightshade' had a flower very much like a potato flower, only very much smaller, and the berries hung in red clusters; it was supposed to be very dangerous. Later on I learnt that the true Deadly Nightshade was a very different plant and considerably rarer than our common Woody Nightshade. Bryony berries were also supposed to be poison; but they looked very pretty as they hung along their vines in the winter hedges in clusters like crimson grapes.

The first flower to appear on the river was the water ranunculus, which grew in great masses on every shallow and sent up its floating leaves in spring to bear aloft the white and yellow-centred flowers. These lovely little white cups came out in thousands just about the time the first swallows arrived and gave a very bright appearance to the river which was welcomed after its long period of winter drabness. I liked this plant very much; both when in flower and when in its flowerless state its long, hairlike masses of leaves swung back and forth with the push of the stream; the green of it was such a rich colour and its never-ceasing movement so graceful. Not knowing its proper name I called it 'Horses' tails' because the long waving green masses so much reminded me of the tails of horses. Later on the still pools were covered with the bright yellow cups of the water-lilies, purple loosestrifes stood in brilliant bunches along the banks and forget-me-nots and bright blue skullcaps peeped between the stems of reds and rushes. In the low-lying boggy spots yellow flags grew in thick masses; there was one very good group of these handsome plants beside the river in Long Ground and, though the approach was treacherous and the river there looked deep and forbidding, it was to this spot that I always went when I wished to gather some of the flowers. In the ditches arrowheads thrust up their three-pointed leaves and loose heads of pinkish-white, dark centred flowers; there also grew water plantains with leaves much the same as the common plantains of the roadsides, but with delicate purple blossoms growing in a widespread, irregular head. Here and there along the bank of the river grew a beautiful pink flowering rush. This lovely flower was not at all common and perhaps because of that its loveliness attracted more careful attention; I do not suppose that the average would have been more than one plant to every quarter mile of river; indeed, on reconsidering this I am inclined to think that half a mile would be a very liberal allowance. Yellow loosestrife could also be found in certain parts beside the river; but this also would have to be classed as a rather rare plant for the district. I once found a specimen of the yellow balsam growing amongst the waterside herbage just below the bridge. My book said that the plant was only found in Yorkshire and Westmoreland and I was therefore pretty pleased with my discovery. Amongst the watercress grew the brooklime, said to be a poison. All the watercress gathered by us was carefully inspected for this plant and for the leaves of water hemlock, which was also said to be a poisonous plant. Most of our watercress was obtained from a winterburn, a stream that ran deep and clear all through the winter and early spring; but which dried up completely during the summer. The banks of this stream were very steep and we collected the watercress by pulling it out with a wooden hayrake. Father usually came with us and did the raking whilst we picked off the tops and packed them into our baskets. Once an eel was raked out with the cress and I managed to catch it after a good many attempts. Along the banks of the ditches and in many places along the banks of the river comfreys hung their close bunches of tubular flowers; sometimes white, sometimes purple. Tall willowherbs were also frequent in almost every damp spot. They were called 'Codlins-and-cream,' which name I suppose originated because of their colour; but their deep pink reminded me more of roses and 'Rosebay,' the name given to another variety found sometimes in the brakes on the downs, seemed to me to be more appropriate.

The predominating flower of the meadows was the buttercup. I believe that buttercups are not considered of any value in a meadow, in fact, rather the reverse; but these meadow buttercups were certainly a lovely sight when they were in full bloom. The meadows then were just unbroken stretches of pure, golden yellow. But before the smaller meadow buttercups came into flower, the greater and deeper yellow flowers of the kingcups glowed out from amongst the dark, shining leaves of the plant in every damp spot and beside the ditches and river. Ladies' smocks, or cuckoo flowers were plentiful in the meadows, as also were ragged robins and, when these plants had passed the best of their season, great white oxeye daisies studded many of the meadows with their conspicuous discs. In Higher Ground and several meadows beyond that little field cowslips were plentiful. Every spring we went out to gather cowslips and, on our return home, we were kept busy for a long while arranging some in vases, hanging the heads of others on strings to make cowslip balls and pulling out the blossoms of others to make a cowslip pudding. A cowslip pudding which is a boiled suet pudding flavoured with the finely-chopped flowers of cowslips, was greatly enjoyed. I have often thought that a pudding made with clover heads would be equally delicious.

Quite different flowers grew in the cultivated fields. Not only were they flowers suited only to a dryer situation, but they were usually annuals only and most of them were small. Heartsease was common and so was fumitory. The heartsease seemed to like the corn crops; the fumitory was more frequently found amongst roots or potatoes. Speedwells and pimpernels also cloud blue and scarlet in the stubbles after harvest. There were often several acres of trifolium which, though a cultivated plant grown as a fodder crop, had a very decorative flower. The great mass of colour when the crop was in full bloom was very rich and reminded me of a deep red velvet curtain. Poppies were not very plentiful on the farm. Father said that they indicated a poor soil and our soil was never allowed to get poor. In the permanent pasture at the end of the garden there were always a few 'cornflowers,' as we called chicory. This plant, with its sky-blue flowers has always been a great favourite of mine; a year or two ago I tried to grow it in my garden, but was unsuccessful.

The roadside hedges produced a very bountiful crop of flowers. Father always remarked on the first of each species as he saw it and I expect this had a great deal to do with the interest I have always taken in wild flowers as an integral part of our country; though as a botanist I am profoundly ignorant. Violets and celandines were usually the earliest. There were three types of scented violets: dark blue, white and a purplish pink. The paler blue, scentless dog violets blossomed later. Periwinkles were also early flowers, and there was the 'mock violet,' as we called ground ivy, because it so often deceived us when we were hunting alone the banks for the other sweet-smelling flower. As the season progressed an increasing variety of flowers decked the hedges. Bluebells, purple orchids and 'Star of Bethlehem,' which was our name for the greater stitchwort, were always first seen at about the same time and usually together. Red campion, or 'Robin Hoods,' came a little later. White campion was not usually found much before harvest time and bladder campion slightly later still. Stinking iris were fairly plentiful; but were not touched because of their objectionable smell and reputation as being poisonous. In the roadside gutters the silverweed spread its fern-like, grey-green leaves and displayed its soft yellow flowers. The flowers of the great mulleins were very like those of the silverweeds; but, instead of growing almost flat with the ground, they were arranged all the way up very tall and stout stems. The leaves of the mulleins were soft and downy. We called them 'pussycat-ears' and always stroked them to feel their plush-like hairness. Foxgloves also were long stemmed, though neither so stout nor so strong as the mulleins. Teasels had to be examined because the curious cups at the bases of the leaves where they joined the main stem always held water and often the drowned bodies of various insects. Toadflax, which we called wild snapdragon, was common everywhere; but was never picked as it wilted so quickly. There were white, yellow and pink dead nettles; but they excited no interest except that it was observed that the bumble bees were very fond of the white-flowered species. There were several sorts of purplish red flowers somewhat resembling the dead nettles, Woundworts and others, which had no known names and were of little interest. Yellow composite flowers were very numerous; but very few were known by any name and most of them were usually referred to as 'sorts of dandelion.' The herb Roberts were 'wild geraniums' and I do

FLOWERS

'The roadside hedges produced a bountiful crop of flowers.'

not remember that any distinction was made between the several sorts that could be found in plenty in the hedges, except that they were 'Kind of geraniums.' In the latter part of the summer mallows were looked for when they had ceased flowering so that we might eat the 'cheeses,' the green seeds. The location of most of the plants was well known, so that we could go straight to them and hunt them over for the seeds; there was one good clump close to the barn which was a regular source of supply. Primroses were fairly plentiful in the hedges; but the High Wood was the favourite spot for them and we had a day there every year, usually on Easter Monday, to gather them. Father was with us on one of these out-ings and, as he was strolling along outside the wood casually poking his stick into the bank beside him, he heard the ferrule strike metal. He dug into the soil and unearthed a small Roman coin. He then explained to me that the country had at one time been occupied by the Romans. Father was very interested in antiquities and had collected quite a number of old coins which had been found by the men whilst ploughing. His source of reference was a large illustrated book in two volumes known as Old England. It was in the High Wood that we also found the wood anemone, and 'Shamrock' which we later knew as wood sorrel. The Shamrock was shown to us as the emblem of Ireland, from which country we were said to have originated many ages earlier; the family tradition was that we were directly descended from the ruling clan in West Ireland, that we had come to England with the ancestors of our own landlord and that we had assisted one of his ancestors in an historic siege against the Roundheads. I have always preferred to let this remain as a pleasant family romance

189

rather than make any attempt to verify it and probably destroy the illusion. I think that, if the wood sorrel had been introduced to us by its proper name, we might have been slightly confused; since we knew the little dock-like sorrel of the fields and meadows and often picked and ate its rather bitter leaves. Our hedges were well supplied with climbing plants, the most conspicuous of which were honeysuckles, Dog-roses and old-man's-beard; the latter, when in seed, was so plentiful in places that the hedges looked as if they were smothered in snow.

A very charming and much-loved flower was the germander speedwell, known to us as 'bird's eye.' The clear, brilliant blue of this little flower was rarely passed unnoticed. I believe the name by which it was known to us was not merely local; but was used as a country name for the flower over a very wide area. When I asked why it was so called, I was told that it was because it was like the eye of a bird; but, although I could see that resemblance, I could not agree that it was a good name, because nearly all eyes of birds that I had seen had been dark in colour: browns, reds and blacks chiefly. A few, like the pigeons and hawks, had bright yellow rings round the dark pupils, and jackdaws and jays had light grey rings; but none had been coloured bright blue. So I secretly named it 'bright eyes' and thought no more of it as in any way connected with birds, but as just a flower-eye that looked at me out of the green tangle of the bank.

There were two sorts of bedstraws very common in the hedges, the white and the yellow. The bloody-nosed beetles seemed to like these plants and could often be found crawling slowly over the thick carpet of blooms. I do not remember being told at that time the legend connected with the yellow bedstraw explaining the origin of its second name 'Lady's Bedstraw,' nor do I think that this name was ever referred to: but the name Bedstraw seemed quite appropriate, as the sweet scent and cushion-like appearance of the plant suggested a comfortable and fragrant couch. Sweet woodruff, a plant somewhat resembling bedstraw in appearance but more upright in growth, could be found in some of the woods. Someone quoted 'sweeter when crushed' and ever after that we picked a spray and pressed it between the leaves of a book. The dried and flattened plant threw out a delicious scent every time the book was opened.

Wild vetches were plentiful, but only the crowded heads of the purple bush-vetch attracted any attention. The little bright yellow Lady's Slippers were often looked for and picked because of their supposed resemblance to satin slippers. I could never see a resemblance; but I kept this to myself. Looking back I realise that I rarely accepted anything just because I was told it; I had to prove it for myself. I find that I am still much the same in this respect.

When the plantain heads began to ripen at the end of summer, we gathered bunches of them to take to an old French lady, a friend and I believe a former teacher of my mother, who lived in the market town and who had several pet cage birds. We sometimes had tea with this lady on market days when one or other of us would be taken to town as a special treat.

Certain flowers could be found only in certain spots. Wild snowdrops grew on an island about two miles up the river. Daffodils were found in a copse on the further side of the Park. Bluebells (wild hyacinths), though scattered in many places in the hedges, grew in much greater profusion in a copse at the back of the dairy house. Harebells were not seen until one approached the downs; they were very plentiful on the downs themselves and nodded their heads in the breeze in company with the curiously knobbed 'Wig-wam' grasses. A thistle peculiar to the downs had a stalk-less flower and its leaves spread out in a circle flat on the ground. One always seemed to sit on one of these prickly plants whenever one attempt-ed to sit down on the turf. Another thistle peculiar to the downs was the everlasting thistle (the carline thistle) which often carried its dull yellow head right into the winter. Thistledown was a regular feature of the downs, where these soft, fairy-like objects might often be seen dancing over the ground in clouds. In the copse in which we used to go nutting we always looked for the bright yellow cups of the Creeping Jenny. I expect there were a good many orchids in the district; but I can only remember two. The common purple orchid was very plentiful in the hedges, partic-ularly where bluebells grew, and up on the downs one could find the curi-ously shaped bee orchid.

The flat tufts of flowers of the large variety of plants similar to the cow-parsley were never named; but they were always examined with interest because of the great variety of brightly coloured insects to be found on them: the red soldier beetles could always be seen on them, as well as many other beetles and flies that seemed to be found nowhere else. Some flowers, such as agrimony, were noticed because we found a peculiar plea-sure in taking their stalks between our fingers and with one quick move-ment ripping off all their seeds. Plantains also were often treated in this manner. Burdocks furnished clinging missiles to throw at each other and often resulted in trouble when one of these little hooked seed heads became entangled in the hair of one of the girls of the party. I notice that other children delight in stripping the seeds from agrimonies and plantains, and throw burdock seedheads at each other.

I have often thought I should like to go again to my old home and walk in the lanes and look at the flowers. I am sure I should find many that I have forgotten. I should also like to lean over the bridge, to see if there are still perch under the second arch, or a pike in the still pool and perhaps a shoal of roach in the last and deepest pool. Then I should look upstream and scan the shallows to see if there were any dace and gudgeon there. I don't think I should care to walk in the fields; I might see too many alterations. It is not always wise to return to scenes of past delights; this often results in disappointment.

For many years I dreamed that I would one day go back to my old home and end my days there; but since then I have found that one's ideas change as one grows older and that no place remains the same. Passing by the farm in middle age I noticed that the house seemed remarkably small and the windows very dark and diminutive according to modern ideas; the rooms also must have been extremely low. Many of the privileges also were gone. The fishing had been let to two Angling Societies, the bridge marking the dividing line. I daresay I should not have found it as comfortable and pleasant as I had thought to live there again. I have also since realised, and wish I had done so at the time, how extremely lucky I was to have spent my early years in such surroundings. To take the fishing as one instance; what would I not now give to be able to angle in water where roach of under half a pound were considered not worth wasting time about and ten pounds weight of fish nothing particularly unusual as the result of a couple of hours' fishing. I feel now that I have been well repaid if I can bring back three roach weighing a pound and a half as the result of three or four hours by the river. I also wish I had known what advantages I then had in time and opportunity for observing the habits of wild creatures. I certainly laid a fairly good foundation; but I know now that I was sometimes rather too hasty in my conclusions. I have since noticed, for instance, that cuckoos do sometimes open their beaks when they call; so it was just as well perhaps that I did not say too much about my imagined discovery that everybody else was wrong in this matter.

1 White Mill Bridge
2 The Camp
3 Eyebridge as it was

Editor's note:

The following articles on White Mill Bridge and The Camp appeared in H. S. Joyce's book *By Field and Stream*, which itself was a compilation of magazine articles.

The third article on Eyebridge at Cowgrove appeared in the *Dorset County Journal* (October – December 1948).

ABOVE: *H.S. Joyce's sketch of the ruined church of Knowleton.*
BELOW: *White Mill Bridge*

1

White Mill Bridge

T is certainly one of the most beautiful bridges in the south of England. It has been stated on authoritative opinion that the lower part of the masonry is twelfth-century work[19], and mention of the bridge is made in the Will of Richard Bryan, dated 1341 (wherein he leaves three shillings for the repair of this and two other bridges in the neighbourhood), mentioning it by its present name and thus clearly showing the antiquity of the Mill also. Its eight ribbed arches span the Stour at a point about midway between Blandford and Wimborne, and connect the parish of Sturminster Marshall with the roads leading to Badbury, Shapwick and Wimborne. Some years ago a movement was started to have the bridge modernised and enlarged to permit of heavy traffic, as it was becoming unsafe. Fortunately the County Surveyor had a mind for beauty and antiquarian interest, as well as for commercial conveniences, with the result that the bridge was repaired and strengthened by a reinforced concrete roadway and closed to all but ordinary vehicular passers. At the re-making of the roadway the surface was lowered about nine inches, thereby increasing the height of the parapet, which formerly stood at two feet six inches. It always made me nervous when travelling over the bridge in a vehicle to look down at the river, with only such a slight protection on either side of me. The roadway is but twelve feet in width; quite sufficient in the old days; but when wagons took the place of pack horses many wordy altercations arose between the drivers should two loads happen to meet on the top of the bridge. It is no easy matter to back a three-horse load of flour or corn down the steep approaches to the bridge, and each driver was positive that it was the other fellow's duty to have first seen that the coast was clear before pulling up on to the bridge. Strong

---

19 An estimated construction date of 1175 makes this the oldest bridge in Dorset. It is regarded as a fine example of solid Norman construction and is rare in that it has remained more or less in its original condition while most bridges have been widened for modern traffic needs.

buttresses stand between each of the arches, both upstream and down; and above the arches the stonework projects a few inches in a straight line and is supported by stones projecting to the same level and placed at regular intervals; this, with the appearance of the outside rib of each arch set back a little from the face of the arch itself, gives a pleasing effect to the structure, reminiscent of the overhanging houses of the Middle Ages. The material consists of warm red sandstone similar to that employed in the structure of the village church at Sturminster Marshall, and also in parts of the Minster at Wimborne; it was probably quarried in the heath country around Lytchett Matravers.

Artists frequently visit the bridge, and I have seen it sketched from a dozen different points of view. Many a time as a boy have I laid in the grass and watched a painter at work on his canvas or paper, and perhaps interested him as much with my prattle about the life in the fields and on the river around there as he interested me in the skill with which he copied the view before him.

Anglers, and those interested in fish, always stop in passing to look down into the clear waters. The arches nearest the Mill usually shelter some good perch that may be seen at times searching close to the watermoss growing from the stones, and devouring the freshwater shrimps that swim about between the swaying fronds, or chasing the minnows that abound on the shallows above. There used to be a fine shoal of roach in the deepest pool – the one nearest the village and known at White Mill Hole. I took my first two-pound roach from that pool; one might often see a pike motionless against the weeds, and watch it dart out and seize some unfortunate dace or roach. The pike had little peace during the summer, for several of the labourers had wire snares attached to long cords which were tied to ash poles, and with these they would noose the pike and haul them up over the parapet. But in winter one could usually get a run from one on a spinner in the deeper holes. I have on several occasions seen great salmon pass up under the bridge. The Stour is not considered a salmon river; but, judging by the numbers that I have sometimes seen dead, I am inclined to think that in suitable seasons some dozens at any rate pass this point on their way to take up positions for spawning on the shallows. I have seen as many as six at one time busy on the shallows there, and many more probably pass by to stations higher up the river.

The luxuriant beds of reeds and rushes shelter many interesting birds. From the top of the bridge one can sometimes look down into the nests of coot and moorhen, and count the eggs; and throughout the spring sedgewarblers and reedwarblers chatter ceaselessly all day long. Even at night a stone pitched into a bed of rushes will immediately start the warblers roosting there into a scolding protest. Martins put up mud nests against the ribs beneath the arches; but frequently the sparrows discover them and, turning out the rightful owners, deposit therein their own grey-speckled eggs. I hated the sparrows and their pushing ways, and made a point of taking every egg in these stolen nests. Kingfishers, also, are often seen passing under the arches, but they rarely stay to fish close by the bridge; they prefer the overhanging willows in the meadows below, or the quiet backwater above where the old mill-hatch used to stand.

About eight or ten miles across the downs stand the ivy-covered ruins of a small church. A story is told that the natives of Sturminster Marshall, requiring a new bell for their church, coveted one from the church at Knowleton. One night in winter a party set off with horses and a cart to steal the bell, and as the ground was covered with snow and the better to cover their tracks, they reversed the shoes on the horses feet. All went well until they reached the bridge on the return journey, when suddenly down the hill behind them came a party of horsemen. Unable to flee with the cart and their prize, they tipped the latter over the parapet of the bridge into the pool below. Some time afterwards, when the hue and cry had died down, they went to the pool to recover the bell; but an old crone, considering the theft of the bell an act of sacrilege, cast a spell over it, so that, though they got it to the surface several times, it always eluded them and slipped back again at the last moment. It is said to be there still, and Sturminster Marshall church bells are supposed to chime-in the local dialect –

> 'Knowleton bell
> Is a'stole
> And drowned in-
> To White Mill Hole.'

How much of the story is true I do not know; but I believe it is a fact that one of the bells of Knowleton church was removed by unauthorised persons and taken elsewhere. But what does it matter? The story is a good one, and such a quaint and beautiful old bridge deserves a little legendary history.

'The thistles attracted common goldfinches'

2

The Camp

T lingers in my memory as a place of mystery, sunlit hours and pure breezes. As children we looked upon it with a sort of reverence. We knew every point on the roads in the surrounding country from which, by reason of the absence of hills, hedges or trees, it became visible, and never failed to keep a look-out on approaching these spots in order not to miss a view of our favourite landmark. It was the nearest point to our home from which the sea could be seen, and the sea was ever a thing of wonder to us who lived a dozen miles inland; a wonder, the sight of which, always brought excited exclamations to our lips: 'The sea! The sea!' As the circle of our knowledge of the country around us widened with our growth, we discovered that the place was looked upon as a landmark very much further afield than we had at first imagined. Just at first we were inclined to resent this; we had for so long regarded it as peculiarly our own that we refused to admit the right of strangers to share in its wonders. We, however, took some consolation when we discovered that most of these strangers only knew of it as a conspicuous feature in the landscape; its hidden treasures and mysteries still remained our particular secret. We were jealous also of our knowledge, and spoke to no one of the fairies that lived beneath the furze bushes and whose dancing-rings we had discovered on the surrounding downland; nor that the Ancient Britons once dwelt there; nor of the ravens. Father told us something of the history of the place, and this we altered and added to according to our own observations and imagination, until every bramble bush and tree became wrapped around in a cloak of history, legend and fancy, much of which was very different from the original story.

The Camp lay upon the crest of the downs about two miles from our home, and consisted of a series of circular ridges, the outermost of which was said to be a mile in circumference. At the highest point in the centre stood a clump of tall trees, mostly pines. It was in these pine trees that the ravens nested. We were told that they had nested there for hundreds of years, and that legend linked them and their prosperity with the continuance of the house of the Lord of the Manor[20]. A raven to us was definitely above the status of an ordinary bird; it was said to live for more than a hundred years, a characteristic in itself quite sufficiently remarkable to place it in a class of its own. It was also associated with numerous old sayings; a bringer of good or bad luck, according to the circumstances. All these things created in our minds the belief that ravens, and our ravens in particular, were creatures possessed of power and knowledge superior in some directions to that of human beings.

Should anyone have asked us about the Camp, we might have answered that the Ancient Britons once lived there behind great wooden fences set up on the tops of the rings, that they fed their flocks and herds on the surrounding downs, and that when wolves or enemies approached, they drove their sheep and oxen into this fort and defied the enemy with clubs and spears of chipped flint. We often formed ourselves into parties of imaginary wolves and barbarians, and carried out attacks and repulsions upon the slippery slopes of the great circles. We believed that it was these same Britons who first dug the dew pond within the inner ring, and that they were eventually driven out from their stronghold by the more powerfully armed Romans. We had seen flint arrow and spear-heads that had been found in the surrounding fields, and father himself had unearthed a Roman coin in the bank of the High Wood that adjoined the Camp. We made several annual visits to the place. The earliest primroses bloomed in the High Wood; the bramble brake produced the earliest and most delicious blackberries; cowslips nodded their golden heads on the downs, and provided us with the main ingredient of a seasonable pudding and materials for delightful, sweet-scented balls. Our friends met us there each summer for a picnic: an incident eagerly looked forward to, but rendered doubtfully pleasant by reason of the innumerable ants that invaded our food, and the minute, but ubiquitous thistles, that made sitting down upon the turf a distinctly uncomfortable proceeding. As we grew older our visits to the place became more frequent as the distance from our home became an obstacle easier to surmount. We wandered there in search of orchids that flowered there in chosen spots: the richly-marked bee orchid and occasionally the white and fragrant butterfly orchid. Butterflies also drew us

---

20 Interestingly, the ravens have since gone from Badbury Rings, as have the Bankes family as 'Lords of the Manor' from Kingston Lacy House.

'Wintry weather'

thither when the craze for collecting was upon us; several varieties of Blues were to be found there in scores, and many others, rare elsewhere, could always be seen in season on the downs. All through the year birds of peculiar interest dwelt there. The wheatear came in spring, and flew from molehill to molehill, flirting his tail and displaying his white rump-feathers in the hopes of drawing the intruder from the disused rabbit hole in which his fawn-coloured mate had deposited her pale blue eggs. The thistles that grew in great quantities wherever their fluffy seeds could find lodgement, attracted numerous goldfinches that were always a delight to watch. Nuthatches, treecreepers and woodpeckers inhabited the ancient oak wood in the depression on the north side of the rings. Nightingales were common in the High Wood and in the thicket surrounding the Park half-a-mile away; so common, in fact, that I remember counting thirteen singing at one time at noon on one occasion. Once a pair of peregrine falcons made it their headquarters, and many a time have I seen them working in unison to defeat and capture one of the innumerable woodpigeons that haunted the fir tree clump and the beeches of the high wood. A heron once nested there, but died on her eggs. Most years saw a brood of wild ducks reared in the brake, from which they were conducted at earliest dawn across the down and along the road to the river nearly two miles away.

As we grew to adult stature, the gun added a further interest to our visits. Wonderful days we have had with the rabbits in the bramble brake. A pheasant, also, would sometimes be found, though the rattle of an old cock springing up from a thicket frequently so startled us that a miss was the result. Most seasons provided a woodcock. Hares were more often found in the outlying gorse clumps or upon the open down itself; they and the rabbits did not appear to live in too close proximity to each other.

There was no better place for miles around from which to view the hounds. The High Wood was an almost certain find. One had only to walk along the ridge of the outer ring to keep the hunt in view for many a mile. I have seen more than one fox jump up in the bramble thicket when we were after rabbits, and one got very much mixed up in the long net outside, before it eventually scrambled clear and streaked away across country with our yelping, panting pack of terriers at its heels.

'Tis a long time since I stood upon the ancient earthworks of Badbury Rings, and I expect many changes have taken place. But no doubt the silver Stour still sparkles in the valley below, with Hardy's[21] tower above the trees beyond; no doubt the white pinnacles of the Needles can still be seen gleaming in the sun on a clear day, and one can still look into the heart of the County, and perhaps even across the border into Wiltshire, from the northern side. I expect also that the mysterious fragment of raised beach still exists beneath the turf where my prying stick discovered it ten years ago, whilst lazily resting beneath the pine clump during a day's shooting with an old schoolfellow.

---

21 The tower in Charborough Park, which features in Thomas Hardy's novel Two on a Tower, can still be seen from the avenue of beech trees at Badbury Rings.

Rabbits feeding

Mallard under attack

3

Eyebridge As It Was

F you turn off the Julian's Road on the right, halfway between the crossroads and the bridge on the Dorchester Road leading out of Wimborne, you will find a gravel-led track which leads first through the allotments and later, having by now become a simple footpath, takes you pleasantly beside the Stour for a mile until it joins the main road to Pamphill or Cowgrove.

At the spot where the footpath ends there is a trackway, rather muddy at times, but with a dry enough path along the edge for foot passengers, which leads to a ford across the river, by means of which the cattle can reach the meadows on the other side of the water. Just above the broad

Lionel Ward's watercolour drawing of the old wooden footbridge at Eyebridge, about 1890. A modern footbridge is still in place today, 60 years after H. S. Joyce was writing.

H.S. Joyce's 1906 painting of a Spaniel

shallows which constitute the ford, you will see a footbridge. It is a Meccano-looking affair, and if you say that it is efficient you will have said all that it justifies. It is a fairly modern structure and serves the purpose for which it was constructed, which is to enable those responsible for the cows to cross the river to collect them, or inspect them, or open the appropriate gate so that they enter the meadow to which they belong and not one owned by some other dairy owner.

Fifty years ago, before the people of Wimborne had cars to take them further afield, this path along the river as far as Eyebridge was a favourite walk for a summer evening. One could get delightful views of the river, the surrounding meadows and the town itself. At the end of the outward walk came the most delightful picture of all: the view of the original wooden bridge which occupied the same site as the modern, very efficient but much less decorative and pleasing, structure which takes its place today.

Wimborne people not only walked along the river to look at the old bridge; all those who had any ability as artists (and many who hadn't) took their sketching boards and colours up through the meadows and

Heron about to strike

did their best to make a satisfactory picture of the scene before them. I was one of the many and I, then in my teens and doing my best to learn something of the job by attending Mr Gill's classes at the Technical School, tried it in pencil, Indian ink and oils. I may have tried more than these three, I cannot remember; but none of my attempts were of sufficient merit to justify preservation.

But at any rate one person who attempted this subject did produce something worth keeping – Mr. Lionel Ward.

Mr. Ward would probably be the last person to claim any ability as an artist – an extreme modesty has always been one of his outstanding qualities – but I have rarely seen a watercolour, in the old style of pure wash, so delicate in tones or so exact in appreciation of the essential qualities of the subject. Unfortunately, like so many good things just at the moment, the original was for export only; it was, in fact, already framed and ready to be sent abroad as a present to Mr. Ward's son.

Fifty years ago the old bridge was already beginning to show signs of decay and, though it was easy enough to step over the gaps made by the missing planks when one crossed it in daylight, it was not so easy when

207

one came back that way after waiting under the thorns for a shot at wild duck on a winter's evening, as I often did; for it was my father's cows which fed in the first meadow on the other side above the bridge and his occupation of the land which gave me the privilege of going there to try and get a good fat duck.

The End